CliffsNotes™
Managing Your
Money

by Mercedes Bailey

IN THIS BOOK

- ■ Assess your income and spending and create a budget
- ■ Make smart choices about credit and debt
- ■ Develop a savings and investing plan to meet your financial goals
- ■ Reinforce what you learn with the CliffsNotes Review
- ■ Discover more information about personal finance in this book's Resource Center and online at www.cliffsnotes.com

IDG Books Worldwide, Inc.
An International Data Group Company

Foster City, CA • Chicago, IL • Indianapolis, IN • New York, NY

IDG
BOOKS
WORLDWIDE

About the Author

Mercedes Bailey has written numerous articles and books including various texts on economics for educational publishers as well as other financial topics. She is the president of Word Management, a firm that writes and edits print and multimedia materials for a variety of clients.

Publisher's Acknowledgments

Editorial

Senior Project Editor: Pamela Mourouzis

Senior Acquisitions Editor: Mark Butler

Associate Acquisitions Editor: Karen Hansen

Copy Editor: Patricia Yuu Pan

Technical Editors: J. Patrick Gorman; Ellen Rogin

Production

Proofreader: Christine Sabooni

Indexer: York Production Services

IDG Books Indianapolis Production Department

CliffsNotes Managing Your Money

Published by
IDG Books Worldwide, Inc.
An International Data Group Company
919 E. Hillsdale Blvd.
Suite 400
Foster City, CA 94404
www.idgbooks.com (IDG Books Worldwide Web site)
www.cliffsnotes.com (Cliffs Notes Web site)

Distributed in the United States by IDG Books Worldwide, Inc.

Distributed by CDG Books Canada Inc. for Canada; by Transworld Publishers Limited in the United Kingdom; by IDG Norge Books for Norway; by IDG Sweden Books for Sweden; by IDG Books Australia Publishing Corporation Pty. Ltd. for Australia and New Zealand; by TransQuest Publishers Pte Ltd. for Singapore, Malaysia, Thailand, Indonesia, and Hong Kong; by Gotop Information Inc. for Taiwan; by ICG Muse, Inc. for Japan; by Norma Comunicaciones S.A. for Colombia; by Intersoft for South Africa; by Eyrolles for France; by International Thomson Publishing for Germany, Austria and Switzerland; by Distribuidora Cuspide for Argentina; by LR International for Brazil; by Ediciones ZETA S.C.R. Ltda. for Peru; by WS Computer Publishing Corporation, Inc., for the Philippines; by Contemporanea de Ediciones for Venezuela; by Express Computer Distributors for the Caribbean and West Indies; by Micronesia Media Distributor, Inc. for Micronesia; by Grupo Editorial Norma S.A. for Guatemala; by Chips Computadoras S.A. de C.V. for Mexico; by Editorial Norma de Panama S.A. for Panama; by American Bookshops for Finland. Authorized Sales Agent: Anthony Rudkin Associates for the Middle East and North Africa.

For general information on IDG Books Worldwide's books in the U.S., please call our Consumer Customer Service department at **800-762-2974**. For reseller information, including discounts and premium sales, please call our Reseller Customer Service department at **800-434-3422**.

For information on where to purchase IDG Books Worldwide's books outside the U.S., please contact our International Sales department at 317-596-5530 or fax **317-596-5692**.

For consumer information on foreign language translations, please contact our Customer Service department at **1-800-434-3422**, fax **317-596-5692**, or e-mail rights@idgbooks.com.

For information on licensing foreign or domestic rights, please phone +**1-650-655-3109**.

For sales inquiries and special prices for bulk quantities, please contact our Sales department at 650-655-3200 or write to the address above.

For information on using IDG Books Worldwide's books in the classroom or for ordering examination copies, please contact our Educational Sales department at **800-434-2086** or fax **317-596-5499**.

For press review copies, author interviews, or other publicity information, please contact our Public Relations department at **650-655-3000** or fax **650-655-3299**.

For authorization to photocopy items for corporate, personal, or educational use, please contact Copyright Clearance Center, 222 Rosewood Drive, Danvers, MA 01923, or fax **978-750-4470**.

Table of Contents

INTRODUCTION

Like it or not, you deal with money every day. Some people deal with it better than others do. The difference is in their money-management skills. You're not born with these skills; you learn them. And improvement comes with practice.

Because you picked up this book, I know that you're at least somewhat motivated to take control of your financial situation, whether it's a disaster or you just need to exercise a bit more discipline. You've come to the right place! CliffsNotes *Managing Your Money* takes a practical look at many phases of money management. You'll find information that you can use to pursue better management of your money so that it can go further and lead to investments that will provide greater financial security.

Why Do You Need This Book?

Can you answer yes to any of these questions?

- Do you need to learn about money management fast?
- Do you not have the time to read 500 pages on money management?
- Do you have limited funds but high hopes for them?
- Do you need tips that you can use now to improve your financial picture?

If so, then CliffsNotes *Managing Your Money* is for you!

How to Use This Book

How to use this book is really up to you — find the approach that works best for your own circumstances. The important thing is to get started. Unless you do *something* to take control of your money, nothing will happen!

To reinforce your learning, check out the Review and Resource Center at the back of the book. To find important information in the book, look for the following icons in the margins:

This icon highlights suggestions that can save you time and energy and perhaps spare you a headache or two.

This icon gives you a heads-up on potentially dangerous situations. Skipping this information could be hazardous to your financial health!

This icon points out things that are too important to forget.

Don't Miss Our Web Site

Keep up with the exciting world of personal finance by visiting our Web site at www.cliffsnotes.com. Here's what you find:

- Interactive tools that are fun and informative
- Links to interesting Web sites
- Additional resources to help you continue your learning

At www.cliffsnotes.com, you can even register for a new feature called CliffsNotes Daily, which offers you newsletters on a variety of topics, delivered right to your e-mail inbox each business day.

If you haven't yet discovered the Internet and are wondering how to get online, pick up *Getting on the Internet,* new from CliffsNotes. You'll learn just what you need to make your online connection quickly and easily. See you at www.cliffsnotes.com!

CHAPTER 1

SETTING REALISTIC EXPECTATIONS

IN THIS CHAPTER

- Learning how to set realistic money-management goals
- Establishing your financial priorities
- Selecting the best money-management strategies for accomplishing your goals

Managing your money is a skill to be learned, just like learning to play softball or to work with a new word-processing program. As with any other skill, money management takes practice, realistic expectations, and the example and advice of those who have "been there and done that." This chapter is about setting realistic expectations for your finances. Your path to financial security and economic success starts here.

Figuring Out What Your Goals Are

Perhaps you have a vague sense that you want to pay off your debts, start a family, be able to put your children through college, or start your own business. None of these or any other goals will happen unless *you* make them happen.

Achieving financial success isn't a matter of luck. Financial success requires attention, discipline, and sound money management.

Setting financial goals is kind of like going grocery shopping: You go to the store with a sense of what you need or want to buy, but the number of choices, the sales, and the attractive displays may cause you to get sidetracked. Just as a shopping list helps a shopper stay focused, a money-management list can help you get off to a good start.

Take a minute to check off the items on the following money-management "shopping list" that seem important to you. This shopping list can help you figure out your financial goals.

- ❑ Spend less than I make
- ❑ Make good consumer choices
- ❑ Balance my checkbook
- ❑ Establish a good credit rating
- ❑ Know where to get good financial advice
- ❑ Save some money every time I get paid
- ❑ Work out a budget
- ❑ Curb my spending appetite
- ❑ Keep good records
- ❑ Use banking services
- ❑ Distinguish between short-term and long-term financial goals
- ❑ Spend enough time on money management
- ❑ Take personal responsibility for managing my money
- ❑ Pay my bills and taxes on time

How many items did you check? Chances are that you think you need to do all these things. And you do. But you don't need to do everything at once. What you need to do first are the basics. The basic approach to managing your money starts with knowing your financial goals.

In general, your goal is probably financial security. Almost everyone wants financial security. The trouble comes in defining just what financial security means to you. Start right now and complete this sentence:

I will be financially secure when I _____

_____

_____.

You may define financial security as being able to retire at age 65 without worrying about having enough money to live the rest of your life the way you want to. Or you may define financial security as being able to retire at age 50. The definition is up to you.

To get started on the road to financial security, begin to think in terms of the next five years. What can you do in the next five years that will help you accomplish your long-term goal of financial security?

Creating a Five-Year Plan

When you have your goals clearly in mind, they become like building blocks. You can more easily defer some of the things you hope to accomplish in the short term because you know that with proper planning and a longer time frame, those things will happen.

To help sort out your goals, ask yourself where you want to be financially in five years. In Table 1-1, rank each goal in terms of how important it is for you to accomplish it within the next five years. On a scale of 1 to 5, 5 is very important and 1 is not important.

Table 1-1: My Five-Year Goals

Objectives	[1]	[2]	[3]	[4]	[5]
Reduce debt	[ ]	[ ]	[ ]	[ ]	[ ]
Save money	[ ]	[ ]	[ ]	[ ]	[ ]
Buy a car	[ ]	[ ]	[ ]	[ ]	[ ]
Buy a home	[ ]	[ ]	[ ]	[ ]	[ ]
Start an investment program	[ ]	[ ]	[ ]	[ ]	[ ]
Reduce income taxes	[ ]	[ ]	[ ]	[ ]	[ ]
Buy life insurance	[ ]	[ ]	[ ]	[ ]	[ ]
Take a big vacation	[ ]	[ ]	[ ]	[ ]	[ ]
Put kids through college	[ ]	[ ]	[ ]	[ ]	[ ]
Other _____	[ ]	[ ]	[ ]	[ ]	[ ]

Look at the items that you checked in the 5 column. Do you think that it's realistic to try to accomplish all your 5s within the next five years? What do you think you can do in one year? The answers to these questions can help you focus on the important aspects of managing your money.

Setting Priorities

It's easy to want it all — a nice place to live, clothes with logos and labels, a great car, meals at romantic restaurants, vacations, and so on. The list expands so easily. The fact is that you have limited resources. You must work with what you have — not with what you want to have, and not with what you think you'll get next month or next year.

All business managers wish that they had more resources to accomplish their goals — more time, more money, more people, more experience. But *effective* managers are resourceful and use what they have to get the best results. They prove their skills by accomplishing tasks with discipline and motivation — skills that you can develop when you approach money management with the commitment to making do with the money you have.

Managing money to accomplish your goals

Take another look at your five-year goals worksheet. If you selected reducing your debts as a very important goal, you want to select money strategies that will make that goal happen. If you selected both reducing your debts *and* buying a great car, your money strategies have to be different. In fact, you may realize that your resources don't allow you to do both at the same time. One objective will have to take priority over the other.

From Table 1-1, select the three goals that you identified as most important. Now rank those three goals in order of importance:

1. _____

2. _____

3. _____

Do you think that you need or want to make any adjustments to your worksheet? Chapter 2 examines the difference between money needs and money wants in greater detail. For now, stick with what you think you need to accomplish within the next five years.

Now estimate the percentage of your income that you think you'll have to allocate to each of your top three priorities. Does common sense tell you that these percentages are realistic? Pay attention to your common sense; it can become your best friend.

Next, write down what you know or expect your annual income will be this year before and after taxes and deductions.

Your *gross income* is your earnings before taxes and deductions get taken out of your paycheck. Your *net income* is your take-home pay — your earnings after all taxes and deductions. Your net income may seem like a lot of money, or it may seem like a pathetically small amount. In either case, as the manager of your money, you start with this amount.

Think now about the annual increase that you can realistically expect if you stay with the same job for the next five years. In a way, the size of the increases doesn't matter. What does matter is that you accept the realities of your situation and manage your money accordingly.

If you postpone major expenditures (such as a new car or an expensive vacation) now in order to accomplish your highest-priority objectives — assuming, of course, that a major expenditure isn't one of your highest-priority objectives — will you realistically be able to afford those expenses later, given the revenue you expect? Begin to think of adjustments that you need or want to make in your expectations.

Managing your time

Like the old adage says, "Time is money." Deadlines are a fact of both personal and professional life. As the manager of your money, you struggle with many of the same constraints that business managers experience. On the one hand, you wish that you had more time to accomplish your goals; but on the other, you wish that you could see and enjoy the results of your work sooner.

To become a successful money manager, you have to become a successful time manager as well.

Everybody has the same 24 hours in each of the seven days of the week. Yet some people just seem to get more done than others do. Why? Because they have clear goals, good time-management skills, commitment, and discipline. You, too, can put time-management and money-management skills to work in order to accomplish your financial goals.

Quickly review your typical week. Estimate the time you spend working, sleeping, eating, traveling, reading, watching television, shopping, dating or with family, playing, and so on. Which activity takes the most of your time? Is that activity really the top priority in your life? Setting your work aside for a moment, how much time have you set aside for the tasks that will help you achieve your financial goals? What time do you allot to managing your money so that your priorities can become reality?

Take the initiative to set aside half an hour every week (Sunday evening may be good, but find the time that works best for you) to develop your skills as an effective manager of your money and time. Time is one of your most valuable resources.

You can spend that half hour doing any number of things. Consider the following:

- Make a list of your goals for the week.

- Review your out-of-pocket expenses against your budget.

- Read an article on personal finance.

- Call your financial adviser, a trusted friend, or a parent and ask for advice about a purchase or financial decision that you expect to make in the coming week.

- Evaluate your money-management performance over the past week and give yourself a grade. Target one area for improvement.

- Evaluate your time-management skills over the past week and give yourself a grade. Target one area for improvement.

- Find $5 to $25 to set aside in an envelope for a special occasion.

- Identify at least one accomplishment that you achieved as a money and time manager over the past week.

- Compare your goals for the week against the priorities that you set for yourself back in Table 1-2. Make adjustments as needed.

Forming Strategies for Success

Some experts think that setting financial goals is the easy part of money management. The hard part is making those goals happen. The plans you make to accomplish your goals are called *strategies*. The handy thing about strategies is that you can change them.

Your strategies for successful money management can change if you find that they aren't accomplishing their purpose. Just as a business manager has to make adjustments to respond to one problem or challenge after another, you can become skillful in making strategic adjustments to manage your money more effectively.

Although many strategies are available to you as a money manager, at least two guidelines can help you evaluate the success of a strategy:

- Be flexible but focused.

- Learn to live on less.

Be flexible but focused

As a money manager, you want to develop a balance between keeping your goals clearly in mind and responding creatively and constructively to changing circumstances and unforeseen situations. No one can anticipate every event in life. Just when you think that you can save a little more one month, the car needs a repair that you didn't count on. Or perhaps you see an ad in the paper for an item you really need. Although you hadn't planned to make the purchase now, you think that, by doing so, you would save money in the long run.

One of the best qualities of successful managers is good judgment. This is especially true of good money managers. Good judgment relates to common sense. Good judgment and common sense are not part of the school curriculum; you learn them from your life experiences.

Learning from your mistakes can be costly, but it's usually effective. Don't be afraid to change and to try something else if one of your money-management strategies isn't working.

Often, you learn good judgment by the example of others you know and respect. Encourage others to share their stories with you. From their stories about the decisions they've made, you can learn about the importance of being flexible. You'll learn how to keep your eye on your goals while making adjustments for setbacks or unexpected difficulties.

Know that your goals may change as your circumstances change. Be flexible and replace goals that no longer suit your needs and wants. Your strategies may change because of proven successes and failures. Be flexible and make the necessary adjustments. If this approach sounds too vague to be useful now, test it out by asking someone whose judgment seems sound and whose decisions you respect. Ask that person, "Am I being too rigid about (name a goal, strategy, or specific circumstance)?" Or ask, "How can I be more flexible about (name the specific situation)?"

Learn to live on less

The single most important skill you can develop as a money manager is to live beneath your means. You've probably heard this guideline — which is the key to financial freedom — expressed in many different ways: Live on less. Put something away from every paycheck. Save for a rainy day. But people seldom follow this advice.

In the section titled "Managing money to accomplish your goals" earlier in this chapter, you wrote down your net annual income (that is, your income after taxes and other deductions are taken out). Calculate how much you would need to save every month and every year to live on 90 percent of your net income. If doing so seems impossible, think of a business manager who suddenly finds out that the budget for a particular project has been cut by 25 percent. The project still must be completed on time and with the same quality standards. As your own money manager, you can appreciate the flexibility and commitment to your goals that such adjustments require.

If your ultimate goal is to attain financial security, chances are that you won't be able to accomplish that goal on your income alone. The ticket to financial security is to save some of your money by living beneath your means. If you don't save some of your money on a regular basis, you won't have money to invest. Investing is a reliable way to accomplish the ultimate goal of financial security because it allows your money to grow. (See Chapter 7 for more on investing.)

Write This Down!

Before you go on to Chapter 2, which focuses on making good choices about spending, take the time to nail down some strategies:

1. Review your five-year plan. Add to that list of goals any even longer-term goals that you have, such as saving for a child's college education or starting your own business.

2. Decide what you consider to be your most important long-term financial goal — something you hope to accomplish in five years or longer. On a blank sheet of paper, write down this goal and label it Goal A.

3. Write down what you consider to be your most important financial goal for the next two to five years. This is a mid-term goal. Label it Goal B.

4. Write down what you consider to be your most important financial goal for this year. This is a short-term goal. Label it Goal C.

5. Take another look at the money-management goals listed in Table 1-1. Write A, B, or C next to each item that relates to one of your specific financial goals.

6. Make a chart that lists your most important short-term goal and the money-management strategies that will help you accomplish it. Do the same for your mid-term goal and your long-term goal.

7. Put your chart of A, B, and C goals and strategies on the refrigerator door so that you're reminded of them every day.

Classifying each goal as short-term, mid-term, or long-term is important because it provides your financial strategy with direction.

CHAPTER 2

DISTINGUISHING NEEDS AND WANTS

IN THIS CHAPTER

- Distinguishing financial needs from economic wants
- Recognizing the range of choices within the categories of needs and wants
- Making choices that move you toward your financial goals

One of your responsibilities as a money manager is to look at your financial situation objectively. Your objective eye lets you step back from the transactions you conducted in the past and encourages you to look at the bigger picture of your financial situation.

Look at the habits and attitudes that you have developed up to now toward managing, spending, and saving your money. Have you made good choices thus far? As your own money manager, you want to make good choices for your hard-earned money. Making good choices involves distinguishing what you need now, and in the longer term, from what you only wish you had now. This chapter shows you how to do so.

What I Really Need Is . . .

Just what are the necessities of life? And how do these necessities change over time? Certainly, what you thought you needed at age 5 (a bike, a grilled cheese sandwich, a cookie) would not be on your list of perceived needs when you're 15 (a designer shirt, a car, a new CD) or 25 (a trip to Hawaii, money to pay the rent or mortgage, a romantic dinner out).

I'll start with the basics. You need housing, food, clothing, and some form of transportation to get to and from your job and other important places. But the range of choices you have to address those basic needs is staggering. Your cost, in terms of both money and opportunity costs, will vary greatly depending on your financial goals and the choices you make.

Remember

An *opportunity cost* is something you give up to pursue a particular decision. For example, if you decide to leave work a little early and go out to dinner with your family, your opportunity cost involves giving up the extra income you would have earned by working later. If you decide to go to graduate school, your opportunity cost involves forgoing a higher standard of living in the immediate future in hopes of bettering your opportunities later in life.

Housing

Your housing choices might include living at home, renting an apartment, sharing an apartment or home with roommates, or buying your own place. For the sake of example, plug in some numbers for each of these options:

- If you rented a studio or one-bedroom apartment, your rent might be $500 per month.

- If you shared an apartment or home with other roommates, your fair share might be $350 a month.

- If you bought your own place, your monthly mortgage might be $1,200 a month.

- If you took in a roommate or border to share your housing costs, or you took a smaller apartment or bought a smaller house, you could reduce your housing costs.

Your choice of housing depends on what you think you can afford, as well as what you perceive the opportunity cost to be. Take a minute to fill in Table 2-1 and apply the opportunity-cost concept to each housing choice. Plug in figures that seem realistic for each choice listed.

Your perception of the benefit(s) derived from each choice is just as important as the opportunity cost. By adding a fourth column to Table 2-1, you can identify what you think the benefit(s) for each choice are.

Table 2-1:   Monthly Housing Costs

Choice	Money Cost	Opportunity Cost	Benefit(s)
Rent an apartment			
Share housing with roommate(s)			
Buy a condo or house			
Take in a boarder			
Downsize housing			
Other			

What did you identify as the opportunity cost for sharing housing with roommates? Chances are that you mentioned a loss of independence. The opportunity cost associated with the other choices might involve settling for less in terms of the other major expenses in your life. For example, if you choose to rent a fancy apartment, you might have less to spend on a car. The choices you make for the basics depend on what you consider important in order to achieve the goals that you identified in Chapter 1.

To determine what housing situation best suits you and your financial situation (or to make any other decision about your money), follow these steps:

1. Calculate how much your choice will cost in terms of dollars.

2. Determine what percentage of your total expenses this choice represents.

3. Factor in the opportunity costs associated with your choice.

4. Weigh the benefits of your choice against the other available options.

Food

Do you have any idea how much you spend on food each week or month? Are you counting fast-food stops and going to restaurants? Although food is certainly a necessity, you probably shouldn't count restaurant food as a necessity. Dining in a restaurant is usually considered entertainment. Eating out is something you *want* or *enjoy* more than something you *need*.

Use Table 2-2 before making decisions about the money you spend on food. Identify the opportunity costs and benefits for each option.

Table 2-2: Monthly Food Costs and Benefits

Food Choices	% of Total Food Expenses	Opportunity Cost	Benefit(s)
Breakfast out			
Lunch out			
Dinner out			
Weekly groceries			
Other			

Sorting out your food choices and weighing the opportunity costs and benefits helps you make better money-management decisions regarding food. You can see how unwise it is to spend 40 percent of your net income on food when you also need to include transportation and clothing in your budget. And you haven't even introduced all those things that you want and are tempted to consider necessities — such as cable television and Internet access.

Transportation

In the category of transportation, too, you have a wide range of choices. Take a look at the choices you've made in the past to get a better idea of your money-management patterns, and then fill in Table 2-3.

Table 2-3: Monthly Transportation Costs and Benefits

Transportation	% of Total Transportation Expenses	Opportunity Cost	Benefits
Car purchase payments			
Car lease payments			
Gasoline			
Insurance			
Maintenance, repairs, etc.			
Public transportation			
Other			

You already know that owning or leasing a vehicle is the most expensive form of transportation. And within the arena of owning or leasing a vehicle, you have many choices — car, truck, sport-utility vehicle, or motorcycle. You may want the best, but you soon find that you can't afford everything you want. This is where the critical skill of distinguishing needs from wants is crucial.

You may decide that you need a car, for example. The car you choose can range from a top-of-the-line model with payments of $700 a month for five years to a clunker for less than $1,000 total. (I won't make you factor in repair costs for now!) Your choice relates to your goals and the income at your disposal.

Clothing

Clothing costs are harder to deal with. People generally don't spend a fixed amount on clothes each month. However, having to purchase a major item of clothing, such as a coat, could cause a big bubble in your monthly budget if you don't use your good money-management skills.

The choice in clothing is enormous. You have a sliding scale from designer labels to resale shops. You may love to shop for clothes, or you may hate it. Try to separate your love (or hate) for clothes shopping from the opportunity costs and benefits that are specific to clothing items.

Review your clothing costs for the last year: Begin by recalling major purchases. Then estimate the number of times you go into a clothing store every week or month and how much you spend each time you make a purchase. You probably spend more money on clothes than you previously thought. Remember that although clothing is a necessity, you can — and probably do — spend a lot more than you need to.

Adding it up

Use your worksheets to tally the amounts that you currently spend each month on the basics — housing, food, transportation, and clothing. Begin to think about the adjustments you want to make in any of those categories in order to accommodate greater spending (or savings) for any of your necessities. For example, if buying a home is one of your high-priority goals, you can anticipate paying a greater amount for the necessity of housing. A greater commitment to your housing expense may require spending less in another category.

What I Really Want Is . . .

One of the biggest differences between being an adult and being an adolescent is the amount of money you have available for discretionary spending. When you were a teenager, chances are that your parents paid for your housing, food, and transportation. The money you earned, you spent — unless your parents insisted, or trained you in money-management skills, and you saved some.

So fast food, records, tapes or CDs, movies, clothing, and entertainment tickets often become the "necessities" of adolescents. A recent survey of teenagers indicated that 73 percent identified entertainment as their top expense, followed by 64 percent who identified clothes and 55 percent who identified music. But for adults, these items fall into the category known as *discretionary spending*.

Understanding what discretionary spending is

Thinking of all the things you want outside the basic necessities as "extras" may be hard to do, but in the world of personal finance, that's reality. Please take this opportunity for a reality check so that you learn to make the distinction between what you *need* (necessities) and what you *want* (the "extras" in life).

As the manager your own money, you may wish that you had more money available for discretionary spending. And you may be surprised at which goods and services are commonly relegated to the category of "extras." Look over this checklist of items that you may consider as ordinary parts of living. Indicate whether you think each item is a basic need (N) or a discretionary want (W).

_____	Stock pot	_____	Pet
_____	Manicure	_____	Beer
_____	Down comforter	_____	Books
_____	Television	_____	Movie tickets
_____	Internet access	_____	Bread
_____	Vacation in Florida	_____	Videos
_____	Washing machine	_____	Stove
_____	Dishwasher	_____	Wallet
_____	Haircut	_____	Acupuncture
_____	Cologne	_____	Sweater

Count up your Ns and Ws. The list of wants should be far longer than the list of needs. Your needs list might include the haircut, bread, and sweater. Some people would argue that a wallet is a necessity; others might claim that health insurance is a necessity. Still, only about 25 percent of these items can be considered true necessities.

More than likely, the "extras" in your life far exceed your needs. One of the most difficult skills you have to learn as a money manager is how to say no to yourself.

Factoring in the influence of advertising

One of the reasons you may have a hard time distinguishing between economic needs and wants is that advertising does such a good job. You're bombarded with advertising on the radio, on television, on the Internet, in the print media, and on billboards and buses.

The purpose of advertising is to promote goods and services so that the prospective customer psychologically transforms a want into a need. Companies spend a lot of money to create a look, feel, and message that works on your emotions. They test their products and marketing strategies on focus groups and use the feedback to develop even stronger messages for their targeted audience.

One of your jobs as an adult is to liberate yourself from the persuasions of advertising. One way to do so is simply to ask yourself: "Do I *really* need this?" Once you identify something as a want rather than a need, you gain control over the choice whether to buy it.

Making Good Choices

Making good decisions about your hard-earned money is a skill that you can learn while playing the game of DICE. No, you're not going to gamble with your money; DICE is an acronym that stands for

- **D**istinguish between needs and wants
- **I**dentify the opportunity costs and benefits associated with each choice
- **C**hoose items based on your priorities, not on impulse
- **E**valuate your choices

In the beginning, you may make some unwise choices. But as you gain experience as a money manager, your judgment will improve if you continue to use the DICE approach.

D: Distinguish between needs and wants

As the section "All I Really Want Is . . ." explains, you need to get in the habit of distinguishing what you *need* from what you *want.* Our consumerist society encourages you to think that things you wish for are really things you need. Make a declaration of independence and start making those judgments for yourself.

Your needs relate to the list of goals that you developed for yourself in Chapter 1. Which of the following do you consider needs as opposed to wants?

   ___ Housing   ___ Food   ___ Transportation

   ___ Taxes   ___ Insurance ___Savings

   ___ Clothing ___ Utilities   ___ Self-improvement

Chances are that you consider all these categories essential to your financial success and your economic goals. Financial success is a result of the proper ordering of needs and wants, and allocating personal resources accordingly. For example, food is an essential item in every budget. Good money managers curtail the amount of money they spend on this item in order to save for other priorities.

What would you add to your list of essentials? Try limiting your list of essentials to ten items. These will make up your priority list that you'll use later.

Remember

Remember that within each category in your list of essentials, you have a multitude of choices. But limit the range to three: basic, middle of the road, and luxury. After each of your essential items, identify whether basic, middle, or luxury choices will help you accomplish your financial goals.

I: Identify the opportunity costs and benefits

When you make decisions about spending your money to provide for the essentials on your list, turn back to the worksheets on housing, food, and transportation (Tables 2-1, 2-2, and 2-3) that helped you identify your options. For each option, you can name the opportunity cost — what you have to give up to pursue a given option — and the benefit — what you gain by selecting that option.

All these steps may seem clumsy at first, but soon they'll become habit, and you'll find yourself gaining both speed and confidence in identifying the relative benefits and costs of the choices you have. Weighing the relative costs and benefits enhances your skills as a money manager.

C: Choose what's best for you

Remember

Only *you* know your financial goals and economic priorities. Only *you* can make money-management decisions that help you achieve your personal goals.

Knowing what's best can seem difficult or confusing. That's why having your list of priorities close at hand is worthwhile. In Chapter 1, you wrote down long-term Goal A, mid-term Goal B, and short-term Goal C. Is that list still on your refrigerator door? Now make a list of your ten most essential economic needs. Next to each category on this list, write B for Basic, M for Middle of the Road, or L for Luxury to indicate what you think you'll be able to afford. Post this list on the refrigerator door as well.

Refer to these lists whenever you must make a decision about your essential economic needs. Obviously, choosing what's best for you involves selecting the option that's most in line with your stated goals.

E: Evaluate your choices

The way to continue making good money choices is to review your choices in terms of how they get you closer to your financial goals. Learn to reward positive behavior. Learn from the mistakes of poor choices as well. Both kinds of choices can develop your money-management skills.

Following are a few ways to reward yourself for sound money management:

■ Pat yourself on the back by doing something you enjoy — take a walk, enjoy a hot bath, spend some time in your garden, or sign up for an inexpensive art, cooking, or dance class.

■ Share the good news — tell a friend or family member about your choice and why it feels good in terms of your priorities.

■ Make a donation to a charitable organization or cause that you support. Keep receipts of these donations so that if you itemize on your tax return, you can take a deduction.

■ Follow the DICE approach for another major purchase and feel good about how much better you are becoming at making wise choices.

CHAPTER 3

PUTTING TOGETHER A BUDGET

IN THIS CHAPTER

- Starting with your real income
- Tallying your expenses
- Working with a personal budget

Imagine trying to sail around the world without a map of ocean currents and winds. Imagine trying to build a house without a blueprint. Imagine trying to manage your money without a budget. All three are equally impossible.

Making a personal budget and reviewing it regularly yields many benefits. First, a budget gives you a sense of direction and control over your personal finances and your economic future. Second, a budget helps you make responsible decisions about spending and saving money. Third, a budget helps you think in terms of long-term and short-term goals and how you plan to accomplish your priorities. Fourth, a budget develops your money-management skills by sharpening your abilities to analyze situations and develop creative solutions to problems.

Looking at Your Income

You can earn money in many ways. In the most common scenario, you earn a paycheck from corporate America. When you got your first paycheck, you may have been shocked to see how small it was. That experience may have been your first lesson in gross and net income.

Or you may be a consultant, entrepreneur, or retiree — in which case calculating your income is a little different. Consultants and entrepreneurs look over their contracts to determine gross income and track deductible expenses. Shopkeepers track monthly sales and expenses. Retirees have an idea of their income from the fixed amounts they receive from social security, retirement plans, and investments.

Gross income

Your *gross income* is the total value of your wages and income from other income-producing activities or investments. Other income-producing activities include goods or services you provide that produce supplemental income. For example, if you make quilts or wood products as a hobby and sell them at fairs, the money you receive is counted as part of your gross income. If you cut hair or mow lawns on the side and are paid for these services, that pay is part of your gross income.

In the following worksheet, add up all the sources of revenue from which you derived income over the past year. The total is your gross income. Any of the following may contribute to your gross income:

Wages from a job   _____

Bonuses and gratuities   _____

Gifts   _____

Interest income from
checking and savings
accounts and insurance   _____

Dividends on stocks
and other investments   _____

Sales of hobby items or services   _____

Child support or alimony   _____

Rent income	_____
Tax refunds	_____
Other	_____
Total Gross Income	_____

Net income

Your *net income* is simply your gross income less a variety of automatic and voluntary deductions. Automatic deductions include income taxes, social security taxes, and so on, whereas voluntary deductions are items such as medical and dental insurance coverage and 401(k) deposits. Most paychecks show an itemized list of both types of deductions.

Remember

The key to remember is that your net income is always less than your gross income because of tax deductions and other automatic and optional deductions.

The first and largest automatic deduction is money withheld from your check for taxes. Federal taxes are withheld based on the information you supplied about the number of dependents (or *exemptions*) that you claim on your W-4 form (the form you fill out when you first start a job). In addition, many states withhold money for state income taxes. Some cities and counties also withhold taxes. You have little to say about the size of these automatic deductions.

Another major automatic deduction is the *FICA* amount — the social security deduction that's required by the Federal Insurance Contributions Act. Your employer, who is also required to contribute to your FICA, matches the portion that's deducted from your paycheck.

As for optional deductions, you can choose from among a wide variety. Many employees choose to participate in the company's 401(k) program, if the company offers one.

Participating in a 401(k) plan is an automatic way to save for retirement that reduces and defers taxes. Optional deductions also include participation in individual or family health and life insurance plans, employee stock purchase plans, charitable contribution plans, and pretax flexible spending accounts.

Take a good, hard look at your net income, which is your budget starting point. Your job as a money manager is to make this net income work hard for you by paying for the necessities of life, enabling you to choose some special "extras," and making sure that your financial future is secure.

You're now ready to begin the process of putting together a budget.

Taking Your Monthly Expenses into Account

Table 3-1 helps you put together a budget. Be brutally honest in recording the amount of money you actually spend in each area. After you complete this worksheet, you can think about ways to make adjustments.

Note that some of your expenses, such as your rent or mortgage, are *fixed* — they don't vary from month to month. Other expenses are *discretionary;* the amount you pay varies from month to month. For example, although food is a necessity, your choices affect the amount you spend on it.

In the Need/Want column, indicate with an N or a W whether the item is a need or a want. In the Fixed/Discretionary column, indicate with an F or a D whether the expense is fixed or discretionary.

Some expenses, such as gifts, vacations, clothing, and emergencies may not occur every month. Still, you need to plan for these. Include a category for "Other" if you don't want to itemize the other-than-monthly expenses.

Table 3-1: Monthly Expenses

Expense	Need/Want	Cost Per Month	Fixed/Discretionary
Housing and Utilities			
Rent/Mortgage payment			
Homeowner's/Condo association fees			
Maintenance and improvements			
Furnishings			
Gas, electricity, water			
Phone (include cellular, pager)			
Food			
Groceries			
Dining out (include fast food and snacks)			
Insurance			
Auto insurance			
Health insurance			
Homeowner's/Renter's insurance			
Life insurance			
Disability insurance			

Expense	Need/Want	Cost Per Month	Fixed/Discretionary
Transportation			
Auto loan/lease payment			
Fuel			
Maintenance and repairs			
Public transportation costs			
Personal and Entertainment			
Alcohol, cigarettes			
Books, magazines, newspapers			
Cable television fees			
Charitable contributions			
Clothing and shoes			
Club memberships			
Gifts			
Healthcare (doctors, dentist, prescriptions)			
Hobbies			
Internet access fees			
Professional associations			

continued

Expense	Need/Want	Cost Per Month	Fixed/Discretionary
Tickets to entertainment events			
Vacations			
Other personal and entertainment expenses			
Debt			
Credit cards			
Personal loans			
Student loans			
Other			
Child care			
Emergencies			
Other			
Total Monthly Expenses			

If your expenses are less than your net income, congratulations! You have disposable income to invest in your financial future or purchase some of the extras that you want. If your expenses and income are too close for comfort, or if your spending exceeds your income, you need to make some changes in order to manage your money effectively and reach your financial goals.

Remember

Your *disposable income* is the positive difference between your monthly net income and your monthly expenses.

Fixed expenses

Your *fixed expenses* include housing, food, utilities, transportation, insurance, and savings. Although these expenses are fixed, the amount you spend in each category can vary greatly, depending on your lifestyle and priorities. For example, take a look at how two different people with net incomes of $2,000 per month budget their money for their fixed expenses.

Fixed expenses for Chris, age 27, who lives in a large city:

Rent	$1,000
Transportation (public)	$100
Utilities	$50
Phone	$100
Food	$400
Savings	$100
Total	**$1,750**

Fixed expenses for Pat, age 35, living in a small town with two children:

Rent	$500
Car payment (for 36 months)	$200
Gasoline and auto maintenance	$100
Auto insurance	$50
Utilities	$50
Phone	$50
Food	$400
Child care	$350
Savings	$50
Total	**$1,750**

Chris and Pat spend the same amount for their fixed expenses each month. But you can see that their lifestyles and priorities are different.

Discretionary expenses

Discretionary expenses are those expenses that are not essential. They vary from person to person, but here's a list of typical items:

- Books, magazines, and newspaper subscriptions
- Charitable contributions
- Clothing and hair care
- Interest on credit card payments
- Gifts: birthdays, holidays, and so on
- Health club memberships

- Hobbies

- Home furnishings, appliances, and electronics

- Insurance: life, disability

- Internet access

- Medical expenses, over-the-counter drugs, and so on

- Music, movies, and cable TV

- Phone options: Caller ID, voice mail, and so on

- Pets

- Tickets to entertainment events

- Vacations

The list of the items that compete for your disposable income is formidable, so keep your eye fixed on your financial goals. Put a list of your financial goals and priorities in your wallet or checkbook and look at them every day, and especially when you're about to purchase a discretionary item.

Now you're ready to put together a monthly budget. Take a look at your fixed expenses and figure out which discretionary items are part of your personal list, and enter the amounts in Table 3-2. Be totally honest about the amounts you spend. Only then can you make adjustments that are better suited to your goals and priorities.

Make a copy of Table 3-2 before you fill it in so that you can track your expenses over several months. If you track your actual expenses over a period of several months, you'll begin to see a trend.

Table 3-2:   Monthly Budget for (Month, Year)

Items	Budgeted Amount	Actual Amount
Fixed Expenses		
Housing		
Transportation		
Utilities		
Phone		
Food		
Insurance		
Savings		
Discretionary Expenses		

After you review your anticipated and real expenses for the month, you may be shocked at what you observe. Take a minute to identify the areas where your anticipated expenses were less than what you actually spent. These areas might encompass food and entertainment. Make a list of the adjustments that you can make to keep your spending more in line with your expectations.

Once a month, after you pay all your bills, take out your monthly budget worksheet and plug in that month's numbers. Then take out your worksheet for the coming month and fill in what you estimate your expenses will be. Review the adjustments that you wanted to make and evaluate your progress.

Factoring in the Need for Savings

You probably noticed that on the budget worksheet, savings are included as a fixed expense. Think of savings as your best friend. Allocating money for savings each month is like paying yourself for doing the job of money manager. How much are your services worth?

Forming strategies for savings

Sometimes the only way to save is to cut expenses. And cutting expenses isn't as hard as it may seem. For example, Monica and Joe, a young couple in their 30s, are concerned about their financial future and are dismayed at how little they save. After taking a hard look at their budget, they came up with some strategies for cutting expenses to increase their savings. Table 3-3 shows their money-saving steps.

Table 3-3:   Sample Strategies for Savings

Strategy	Monthly Savings
Take lunch to work instead of going out	$60
Take public transportation to work	$40
Stop smoking one pack a week	$10
Reduce fast-food and restaurant dining by 20%	$60
Total estimated monthly savings	**$170**

By saving this $170 per month, Monica and Joe will save an additional $2,040 in one year. Add in interest, and over the years, those savings will increase dramatically.

Take a minute to identify four ways in which you can cut your monthly expenses to save more money and reward yourself for being a good money manager. Then tally your total savings for the month and figure out your annual savings.

1. _____

2. _____

3. _____

4. _____

Saving for big-ticket items

Imagine that included in your financial plans is something major — such as saving to get married, buy a home, have a child, send a child to college, or buy into a retirement community. These big-ticket items require major adjustments to your budget.

For example, one couple wanted to plan for their first child and decided to eliminate one of their car expenses. They sold one car, cancelled that auto insurance, and saved more than $3,600 in one year. They coordinated travel to work, and the minor inconveniences did not compare to the smile of their first child.

Another couple wanted to move into a retirement community that provided independent living for the healthy through hospice care for the dying. The move required the transfer of $500,000 in assets. They planned to finance this by liquidating their assets by the sale of their home and cars and downsizing their furnishings.

If you take your savings plan seriously — even if you can save $2.74 a day (the approximate price for a cup of coffee and a sweet roll for breakfast) — you can save $1,000 a year. If you invest that $1,000 (see Chapter 7 for more about investing), you can take great pleasure in watching that money grow. You owe it to yourself to ensure for yourself financial security and a comfortable retirement.

CHAPTER 4
DEALING WITH DEBT

IN THIS CHAPTER

- Looking at how people get into debt
- Reducing debt and saving simultaneously

Sooner or later, everyone experiences financial difficulty. This chapter tells you how to avoid unmanageable debt and what to do about debt if you're already there.

Sources of Debt

Common sources of debt include cars, college education, home mortgages, home equity loans, various addictions, and simple overspending. In each case, you need to avoid some pitfalls.

Auto loans

Most people spend more for a car than they can comfortably afford. Before going to a car dealership or answering an ad for a car, do your homework and give yourself time. Buying a motor vehicle on impulse can be disastrous. Smart car buying involves several steps:

1. Go back to the budget that you developed in Chapter 3 and know what you can afford. Think about all the things you need and want to do with your net income and figure out how much is left over for transportation costs.

2. Shop around in the "virtual market" before you step outside your house. Look at car ads in your local newspaper. Go to the Internet and compare prices there. If

you're considering buying (or selling) a "predriven" car, check the published Blue Book value of the particular model. Read magazines like *Car and Driver, Consumer Reports,* and *Money* to learn about expected performance and standard car prices.

3. Narrow down your car choices based on what you think you can afford. Focus on a couple of makes and models. Compare costs in your virtual marketplace.

Be clear about the number of bells and whistles you want to pay for. Cars that come "nicely equipped" carry expensive add-on costs. The cost of a basic model can quickly escalate beyond your comfort level when a dealer shows you the latest gadgets for a car.

4. Name your *bottom line* — the total amount of money you can afford to allocate to transportation costs. To the total cost of each car you've selected in your virtual marketplace, figure in the sales tax or transfer tax, state registration fees, cost of the license, automobile insurance, and the expected fuel costs for the amount of driving you expect to do.

5. Decide whether you can get the best value for your bottom line amount by buying a new car or a used car. If you decide to buy a used car, work with a reputable dealer or a respected individual, check the service records, and always have your own mechanic check out the used car before you buy it.

6. Shop by phone before going into a car dealership for either a new or a used car. Call several dealers that offer the same make and model car that you have decided you can afford. If they won't give you a quote over the phone, be careful. You probably don't want to do business with anyone who can't provide a quote when you ask for it because they can't give their "word." Get two or three quotes. Be sure to compare apples and apples — exact models with the same equipment.

7. Be prepared to haggle. If you don't feel that you have this particular skill, ask a friend who does to go with you. Just make sure that you've done your homework.

Now you face the reality of getting a loan to pay for the car. Most people get financing through a bank, a credit union, or the car dealership itself. Loans for new cars generally charge less interest than the loans on used cars, but they usually require some down payment. In some cases, you can trade in your previous car as your down payment. Some people add some money they've saved to their car's trade-in value in order to reduce the monthly payment costs.

The length of your car loan can vary. Three-year terms used to be common. Now, because of the rising cost of cars, some loans extend for five years. The benefit of these longer loans is that your monthly payments are lower. On the other hand, you pay more in interest, and your budget carries the loan payment as a fixed expense for a longer time.

A college education

College is a lifetime investment, but it's expensive. Consider today's average costs, listed in Table 4-1.

Table 4-1: Estimated Average Four-Year College Costs

Starting Year	Public School	Private School	Fancy School
2000	$41,300	$105,000	$148,000
2004	$52,000	$132,000	$187,000
2008	$66,000	$167,000	$236,000
2012	$83,000	$211,000	$298,000

Don't let the figures deter you or your child from going to college or planning to do so. You can pay for a college education in a number of ways, although most college students do emerge from the experience with some debt. The sources for funding a college education usually include a combination of any of the following:

- **Parents' income:** Parents should share with their children what they are able to contribute to help pay for college. With this information, students know how much additional money they will need to earn or borrow to complete their education.

- **Student savings, work-study programs, and jobs:** Students should save for their own education during high school. In addition, many students work during college to pay some of the costs.

- **Guaranteed Student Loan (GSL):** Student loans are frequently necessary to cover the expense of college tuition. The most common way to help finance a college education is through subsidized federal Stafford loans. After a needs analysis, students can apply for a Stafford loan and borrow specified amounts for each of the four years of college, with the maximum total for undergraduate work not to exceed $23,000. Graduate students can borrow up to $65,000. The loan rate of interest is based on the 91-day Treasury bill as of July 1 of each year, plus 3.1 percent. However, the interest rate has a cap of 9 percent.

  The federal government subsidizes the Stafford loan until six months after graduation. Students are then expected to take personal responsibility for repaying their student loans over a ten-year period. Failure to repay college loans results in a poor credit history.

- **Financial aid:** Most colleges work to put together some sort of financial aid package for each student who needs aid, although the amount may be small. The aid can be a combination of federal support, state money, and scholarships funded by school endowments.

■ **Federal PLUS Loans:** These loans enable parents of students to borrow up to the cost of the entire college tuition, minus any other aid the student receives. The disadvantage is that parents are required to start paying off the loan within 60 days of securing the loan. Students can defer paying the principal of the loan but must begin interest payments within 60 days.

■ **Federal Perkins or NDSLs:** The National Direct Student Loans (NDSL) or federal Perkins loans are directed for special education assistance. They are similar to the Stafford loans in that payments begin six months after graduation, and the entire loan must be paid back within ten years. Students may defer payment, however, if they join the Peace Corps, enlist in the military, or teach in inner-city schools.

Search the Internet for scholarship offers. Literally thousands of scholarships are out there, not only for gifted students and athletes but also for those who are members of other groups or just need financial assistance.

Mortgages

When you think that you're ready to buy a home, contact your personal banker and ask for help in determining the amount of mortgage you qualify for, learning about the process of applying for a mortgage, and calculating how much the bank would be willing to lend to you. Your mortgage will probably represent the largest debt you have. As with all debts, think about this loan carefully and shop around for the best deals. You may also want to shop for loan rates by using a mortgage broker or the Internet.

The bank will explain the mortgage guidelines presented by the Federal National Mortgage Association (FNMA). These guidelines suggest that the total amount of money you spend on mortgage, taxes, utilities, and maintenance shouldn't exceed 28 percent of your gross monthly income. The more debt you owe, the less money is available for a mortgage. The bank will ask you about your current income and your outstanding debts, including student loans, car loan, and credit card debt. The bank will add these figures to the fixed expenses that eliminate income you can allocate for a mortgage.

Often, banks qualify people for a larger mortgage than may make sense for financial planning purposes. It's important to factor in your expenses and savings needs when deciding how large of a mortgage to get.

In addition, the bank will indicate its current expectations for a down payment. Some down payments may be as low as 5 percent, but generally 10 to 20 percent is required. The bank will also indicate the current interest rates on home mortgages and help you estimate your mortgage payments based on the type of home you can afford.

Home mortgages come in two basic types, and both come with 30-year and 15-year repayment options:

■ **Fixed rate mortgage:** This option is the most traditional type. With a fixed rate mortgage, you lock into a specific mortgage rate for the life of the loan.

■ **Adjustable rate mortgage:** Commonly abbreviated as ARM, the rate on this option can go up or down, depending on the current interest rate at the time of readjustment.

If you choose a 30-year mortgage, your monthly payments will be lower than with a 15-year mortgage. However, the amount of interest you will pay over the course of the loan is considerably higher. Ask your banker to calculate the mortgage costs both ways and tell you what the total interest is for a 15- and a 30-year mortgage. (If you want the security of a 30-year rate but want to speed things up so that you don't pay so much interest, consider paying off the 30-year mortgage more quickly by doubling up on payments or paying more than the required monthly amount.)

In addition to the cost of the mortgage, many banks also charge you for *points,* which are add-on charges based on the amount of your mortgage. A point equals 1 percent of the loan's principal. If a bank charges points, the interest rate is generally lower. The longer you intend to own your home, the less impact points have on your total costs.

Home equity loans

Equity is the difference between what you owe on your home and the market value of your home. After you build up some equity in your home and its value has appreciated, you can take advantage of this money by applying for a home equity loan. This line of credit is secured by the equity in your home. The trouble with this arrangement is that if you fail to make your home equity loan payments in addition to your mortgage payments, you can lose your home to foreclosure.

In effect, getting a home equity line of credit is like taking out a second mortgage on your home. Before applying for a home equity loan, consider the following:

■   Do you have the discipline to use the home equity loan only for major expenditures — a new roof, home improvement, or perhaps a college education? Don't use a home equity loan for vacations or other discretionary expenses.

- Can you repay the loan in a timely fashion?

- Are the home equity rates favorable? Because the value and equity in your home secure home equity loans, the interest rates are generally lower than for other personal or commercial loans. Most home equity loan rates are based on the *prime interest rate* (the rate that banks charge their best customers) or on a government Treasury bill rate. These rates vary over time. You have to anticipate your ability to repay in the course of fluctuation.

A major advantage of a home equity line of credit is that, like your mortgage, the interest on this type of loan is tax-deductible. But if you lack self-discipline, a home equity loan is not for you.

Getting Out of Debt

Getting into debt is easy to do. However, you know that you're in trouble when

- You can't pay the entire amount billed on your credit card(s).

- You take cash advances from your credit cards to pay basic bills, like rent.

- You're up to the limit on one or more credit cards.

- You struggle to make your car payments.

- You have been late paying the rent, mortgage, car loan, or other major bill.

- Late fees and bank charges for insufficient funds eat into your available cash.

- Every unexpected expense becomes an emergency, and you don't have money to deal with it.

If you recognize yourself in several of these scenarios, the time has come for serious adjustments. As a money manager, you need to use your debt-reduction tools, which include reducing your spending, increasing your savings, and developing an action plan to reduce your debt.

Reduce your spending

Dealing with debt involves just a few strategies. But all the suggestions that follow relate to one basic tenet: To reduce — or, even better, eliminate — debt, you *must* say no to all the things you wish you had.

Try these ten little tricks to reduce your spending:

- Look at your last credit card bill. Circle all the items you could have done without and add up their total cost. Think of how good you would feel if you could use that money to pay off your debts or put it into savings.

- Remove all the credit cards from your wallet, make a trip to the library, and read an article on money management. When you come home, you'll realize that you didn't suffer major discomfort because you didn't carry your credit cards with you.

- Go to a local store with the intent of spending ten minutes there walking the aisles without making a single purchase, no matter what bargains you find. Visit one store every day for a week and do the same thing. With practice, you'll learn to resist the temptation to spend.

- Look at your car debt. Ask yourself what kind of car you could be driving if your payments were $50 less each month over three years. If you're satisfied with the answer, you can sell your car, pay off the existing loan, and buy something less expensive.

■ Examine your home expenses. What one thing could you eliminate?

■ Ask for the cooperation of everybody in the family. Plan a Sunday evening suggestion night and ask everybody to bring an idea for reducing their spending by 10 percent. Write down all the suggestions and display them on a bulletin board or on your refrigerator door.

■ Examine your food expenses carefully. If you gave up the morning stop for coffee and a bagel, you could reduce your spending by almost $20 a week. Take lunch to work at least one day a week.

■ Brainstorm with yourself and create a list of ten things (large or small) that you personally can do to reduce your spending. Start tackling them immediately.

■ Reduce your daily spending and your overall patterns of spending.

Start saving

Even when you feel that your debts are overwhelming and it takes all your money to just stay afloat, start a savings plan. Many people think that they can't start their savings plans until all their debts are paid off. Wrong! Begin by saving $4 or $5 a day by not buying breakfast or lunch. Put that money into an envelope at the end of every day. At the end of a week, add it up. Write yourself a check for the amount of cash in your envelope at the end of the month and deposit the check in your savings account. Use the money in the envelope to pay for fuel for the car. With this system, you'll soon eliminate the gasoline charges on your credit cards.

Look at the tips for savings in Chapter 6. Surely, you can resolve to master at least one tip. With the discipline of saving regularly comes the discipline of saying no to unnecessary spending. Be prepared, however, to use some — but not all — of your savings to pay off your debts.

Taking action to pay off your debts

Your action plan for dealing with your debt involves communication, commitment, and discipline. When debt gets out of hand, embarrassment is natural, but don't try to cover it up.

The first step in paying off your debt involves communication. If you're married, talk with your spouse — don't argue or blame. Talk about what each of you is willing to do to reduce your debts and start serious savings. Each of you can come up with at least three suggestions that you personally are willing to implement. If you have children, ask them to do the same thing: come up with three things that they personally are willing to do to help the family reduce debt.

Talk with your lenders, your bank, and your credit card institutions. Explain your situation. They'll work with you to arrive at a repayment plan that you both can live with. Remember that these institutions want to see you succeed. Your success is in their best interest because they make money by making good loans.

Remember

Commitment and discipline are essential to your action plan. You must be committed to paying off your debts or getting them to an acceptable level. The hard part comes with the commitment to change the habits and attitudes that got you in trouble in the first place. You also need discipline to pay off your debts. You got yourself into debt, and only you can get yourself out. Start now!

CHAPTER 5

GETTING CREDIT (WHERE CREDIT IS DUE)

IN THIS CHAPTER

- Establishing credit
- Determining acceptable levels of credit debt
- Discovering the pros and cons of paying cash versus using credit

You may remember your first credit card as a badge of adulthood. I remember starting out in search of credit after I got divorced, having had a terrible marital credit history. No one wanted to give me credit, yet I traveled on my job and needed access to credit for travel-related expenses. What could I do?

My first step was to go to my bank and apply for a *debit card*. (A debit card is like a credit card in that you can use it to make purchases, but it's also like a check because it automatically deducts the cost of the purchase from your checking account.) I recorded each debit card purchase in my check register as if I had written a check. A good record with the debit card led to successful applications for credit cards. Then the issue became how to limit my use of credit. And that's the story of this chapter.

The Pros and Cons of Credit

Securing credit is like applying for a loan: You ask a financial institution to lend or "rent" you the use of its money. For the use of the money, you can expect to pay extra money. The terms of your agreement specify the rate of *interest* — the extra money you pay in order to pay back your debt to the institution that issued the credit card.

The benefits of establishing credit are significant:

- The ability to make major purchases when you don't have immediate cash for the item(s)

- A sense of security that you can handle an unexpected emergency by using credit

- The convenience of shopping without carrying a lot of cash

- Monthly itemized credit statements that enable you to track your purchases

- Worldwide acceptance

Warning

But establishing credit is a double-edged sword. With its benefits come some major disadvantages, including the following:

- Easily available credit can make spending become second nature.

- If you can't pay off your credit balances on time, you affect your credit rating.

- You can fall into the trap of paying off some of the credit debt instead of paying the whole amount.

- When you add credit expenses to the stated price, you end up paying more than you expected.

Establishing Credit

When you're fresh out of college, starting over after a divorce, or emerging from bad debt or bankruptcy, your thoughts turn to establishing or re-establishing credit. Here are some tips for establishing credit and getting off to a good start in managing credit debt:

- **Open a checking account and a savings account at a local bank or credit union.** (See Chapter 8.) Keep your balance at the acceptable minimum level, and *never* overdraw your account.

- **Make an appointment with your personal banker to apply for a bank charge/debit card.** Come prepared with a statement of your personal assets and liabilities and your monthly budget.

- **Apply for a charge account at a local store.** Shop at this store and charge your items. Pay the bills promptly.

- **Ask a parent or mentor to cosign for a credit card issued in your name.** With this arrangement, you have personal responsibility for payments, and your credit history will be reported in your name. The cosigner agrees to take on the liability for credit payments on an account if you can't pay.

- **Keep trying.** You might be rejected for one credit card and then granted another, especially after you establish your credit-worthiness by opening bank accounts and successfully using bank cards and store charge cards.

After taking these steps, you're on your way to establishing credit. Now you need to understand the amount of credit you can afford to take on.

Deciding on an Acceptable Level of Credit

When the credit card offers start coming, they seem to compete with each other by raising the level of credit that they will extend to you. You may get a small thrill when you receive a letter from a credit card company telling you that you're prequalified for a line of credit that boggles your mind.

These days, companies are offering $10,000, $25,000, and even up to $100,000 lines of credit. This is absurd! Why would anyone want that much credit card debt? You may be flattered to think that someone would extend you a line of credit for large amounts of money, and you may be tempted to say, "You never know when that money would come in handy." Don't give into temptation too easily — you need to think seriously about the level of credit debt that your income can tolerate. Just because a lender is willing to extend that line of credit doesn't mean you have to use it. Still, the temptation to do so is great, and many fall in the trap of using their line of credit to the maximum.

Imagine Mr. and Mrs. Conservative — the couple who pay cash for everything and don't owe anyone money. Their debts are paid. Their cars and house are paid for. Their children went to college and are now buying houses of their own. Yes, they borrowed money, but only to buy their home, and then they paid off the mortgage ahead of time.

Now, imagine Mr. and Mrs. Bigspender — the couple you like to be with because they always pick up the tab for dinner. They talk about the expensive vacations they take. They live in a large home and drive expensive cars. They're up to their eyeballs in debt. They have no clue about how to change their spending and debt habits.

Your own comfort with credit card debt is likely to be somewhere in the middle. The following worksheets can help you figure out what your level of debt should be.

First, use Table 5-1 to identify the amount of debt you currently carry. The first two lines of the table are examples; fill in your own debts in the remaining lines. (Feel free to add lines if you need to.)

Table 5-1: My Debts and Monthly Payments

Creditor's Name	Loan	Total Due	Monthly Payment	Maturity
State Bank	Car	$5,040	$140	36 months
VISA/Citibank		$1,000	$120	10 months

Total Debt: _____

Total Monthly Payments: _____

Most financial advisers recommend a personal debt limit of between 10 and 20 percent of your net income, maximum. To figure out your personal debt ratio, use the following worksheet.

1. List your monthly net income.   _____

2. To accommodate debt of 20 percent, divide your net income by 5.   _____

To accommodate debt of 15 percent, divide your net income by 6.7.   _____

To accommodate debt of 10 percent, divide your net income by 10.   _____

3. List your monthly debt obligations (see the "Total Monthly Payments" line in Table 5-1).   _____

4. Calculate your *debt margin* (the ratio of debt to net income) by subtracting line 3 from whichever level of debt you're comfortable with (using one of the lines in Step 2).   _____

5. Figure out your personal debt ratio by dividing your monthly debt obligations (line 3) by your net income (line 1).   _____

This worksheet helps you determine the level of credit that's acceptable to you with your net income. If your debt margin (line 4) is too close for comfort, sit down right now and write down three ways that you can reduce your monthly credit installment payments. If your debt margin is comfortably less than your monthly credit obligations, don't rush out to buy things on credit. Instead, congratulate yourself on your frugality and revisit your savings plan (see Chapter 6).

Avoiding the Credit Card Trap

Many financial advisers will tell you never to take your credit cards out of the house. As soon as you do, their easy availability makes frivolous purchases easier and more tempting.

For many people, the stack of plastic in their wallets gives them a sense of security and pleasure. The greater the number of credit cards, however, the greater the danger of overspending. To avoid costly credit card abuse, consider the two-card system, described in the following sections.

Finding a good card

Selecting a credit card that works best for you is often as difficult as establishing credit in the first place. You have so many choices — more than 19,000 financial institutions offer VISA or MasterCard cards. In general, though, credit cards vary in at least four aspects:

■ **Annual fees:** Some cards charge an annual fee ranging from $25 to $75. Some cards waive the annual fee for first-time customers but charge the fee in subsequent years after the customer has become accustomed to using the card. But other cards do not charge an annual fee. Look for these cards.

■ **Interest rates:** Rates vary, generally ranging from 8.5 percent to 21 percent. It pays to shop around and compare interest rates.

Write the Bankcard Holders of America at 560 Herndon Parkway #120, Herndon, VA 22070, and ask for a copy of the publication *Low Interest Rate/No Annual Fee List* ($4). This directory lists the banks that offer low rate/no fee cards.

■ **Grace periods:** Some cards begin to charge interest from the date of each purchase; others begin to charge interest from the date of expected payment. Again, shop around to find a card that offers a longer grace period.

■ **Cobranding:** More and more credit cards are partnering with airlines, gasoline companies, and financial institutions to give customers incentives to use their cards. Some cards give frequent flyer miles on a particular airline for the dollar value of purchases made with the card. Others offer free gasoline or discounts on purchases. This type of card may be advantageous to you, but weigh the interest rates and annual fees against the benefits.

Using the two-card system

After you compare cards, select two that serve your needs and refuse or cancel all the rest. Determine to use one card with the lower interest rate for large purchases because you probably cannot pay off the balance in one month, and the other, with the higher interest rate, for smaller purchases because you will pay off this balance each month.

The two-card system works best when you know that you'll be making a major purchase. Perhaps you know that you need a refrigerator or you want a better stereo system. These are big-ticket items, and you probably don't have ready cash available for the purchase.

Become familiar with the timing of the billing for your large credit card purchases and time your major purchases accordingly. For example, if you make a purchase immediately after the billing date and you have a grace period of 25 to 30 days, you have, in effect, free credit for almost two months. If you buy that refrigerator on February 2, the day after your billing date, the purchase will not appear on your bill until March 1. You often have 30 days to pay without interest. If you pay the entire bill on April 1, you will not have paid any interest for that purchase.

If, however, a finance charge is calculated on the average daily balance with newly purchased items included, finance charges are immediately added to your bill, and it's better to pay the bill as soon as you get it, because the charges add up daily.

Use the second credit card for your smaller purchases. Pay the amount due on this credit card in full each month. Limit your spending to accommodate those purchases that you can pay off entirely and those larger purchases that you can manage while still maintaining the comfortable debt ratio that you identified earlier in this chapter.

Understanding the cost of credit

Credit costs you money. For example, if you use your credit card to buy a $120 watch as a Christmas gift, here's how the costs add up: First, add in your state sales tax. Then add in the finance charge. This charge, in its common usage, means the combination of the interest rate and any transaction fee the credit company adds to single or cumulative transactions. If your finance charge is 19.2 percent and you pay $10 per month for a year to pay for the watch, your watch costs $120, plus sales tax, plus about $15 in credit charges.

Warning

If you decide to leave part of your bill unpaid, the creditor will charge you interest. The creditor also assesses a transaction charge for the service of extending credit to you. The entire finance charge is taken from your payment, and your debt is reduced only by what's left over. For example, if you make a partial payment of $50 and the finance charge is $10, your debt is reduced not by $50 but by $40. Partial payments reduce your debt very slowly.

The more you buy on credit, the more you pay to reduce your debt. You know that you're in credit trouble if you recognize any of the following warning signs:

■ You find yourself charging more and more and paying with cash less and less.

■ You let some bills slide and postpone payment for a month.

■ You make partial payments instead of paying the entire bill.

■ Your debt-to-net-income ratio exceeds 20 percent.

■ You take out new credit cards to cover additional purchases after you max out the cards that you're currently using.

Only *you* can control what you buy on credit. Credit cards that get out of control cost you money and delay your ability to invest in your financial future. Try the following tips to reduce your credit costs:

■ Shop for a low-cost or free credit card.

■ Don't pay extra annual fees for premier cards that offer gold or platinum benefits unless you really need the extra benefits that they offer.

- Use your credit cards only for necessary purchases. Don't charge toys, liquor, or vacations. If you can't pay cash, you don't need them at the moment.

- If you're making a major purchase on a credit card, select a card that charges a lower interest rate. *Barron's* publishes a weekly list of comparative interest rates.

- Review your credit statements carefully each month. Attend to mistakes or questions about your bill promptly.

- Pay the entire bill on every credit card every month.

- Reduce the amount of credit available to you. Cancel credit cards that you don't need.

- Consolidate your credit card debt so that you pay interest charges on only one card.

- Pay off outstanding credit card balances before taking on further debt. Reevaluate the amount of debt that you're willing to carry in relation to the amount of money you want to save.

- Pay off the credit cards with the highest interest rates first.

CHAPTER 6
CREATING A SAVINGS PLAN

IN THIS CHAPTER

- Understanding the role of savings in your financial security

- Motivating yourself with the benefits of a savings plan

- Using less of your resources now to accomplish your long-range goals

Every so often, the newspaper carries a story about an unexpected and generous bequest of some humble benefactor to a hospital or university. The article indicates that the benefactor was a teacher or janitor making a modest amount of money. Somehow, over the years, the individual amassed a great fortune. The story usually indicates that the person just lived frugally and saved a lot. The moral of those stories is that it isn't how much your earn, but how much you save, that makes the difference between financial success and just getting along.

If you didn't develop the habit of saving money as a child and you're tired of living from paycheck to paycheck, this chapter can help you find ways to save. This chapter also explains the benefits of savings, gives you tips on how to save, and shows you what to do with savings after they accumulate.

The Benefits of Saving

Why save at all? Because your savings protect you from emergencies such as major car repairs or even the loss of a job.

Your savings also allow you to make those major purchases, like car or home, that are so important to you. You can also convert your savings to investments that enable your money to grow.

Without savings, you live with financial anxiety. Emergencies are a fact of life — not a surprise that strikes out of the blue. Your savings should include an emergency fund to deal with the "unexpected" disasters such as car repairs, a plumbing snafu, or major dental work. This emergency fund should be left alone and not used for investment purposes.

You have two other reasons to save your money. The first is to make major purchases, such as a house, car, or college education. The second is to make sound investments. Financial experts agree that the way to financial security and a comfortable retirement is to invest money so that it will grow. The money you earn will not grow substantially unless you make sound investments. You will have no money to invest unless you save.

Savings is the key to financial security. Without savings, you will not have money to invest so that your money grows in value and your financial future becomes more comfortable. You can save money in many ways — whether it's by joining a savings plan at work or by creating your own regular savings habits. The important thing is to start saving something.

Savings Plans on the Job

In the early 1980s, Congress passed legislation that led to the creation of savings plans through businesses that are popularly called *401(k) plans*. These plans have become increasingly popular because they encourage employees to save pretax dollars, thus reducing and deferring taxes on income. When you set aside money for a 401(k), this portion of your income is not taxed until you withdraw the money from the account.

Teachers and employees of not-for-profit organizations can contribute to 403(b) plans. State and local government employees can choose to participate in 457 plans. These plans are similar to 401(k) plans in that they allow employees to reduce their taxable earnings by making contributions to retirement savings plans. Because more people participate in 401(k) plans, I'll stay with that example for the rest of this section.

A 401(k) plan is often called a *salary reduction plan* because your contributions are voluntary deductions from your wages. You can choose to contribute up to a certain amount of your pay (the current maximum is $10,000 per year) to the special retirement account that the company has set up with an authorized institution. You never see this money, yet every paycheck indicates the amount of your contribution.

The benefits of a 401(k) plan are numerous:

■ Your contribution reduces your taxable income because you make your contribution with pretax dollars, which reduces your income tax liability.

■ In many cases, the employer contributes to the employee's 401(k) account. In some cases, the match is $1 for every $1 the employee contributes; in others, it's 50 cents per employee dollar.

■ You can choose where to invest your 401(k) contributions within a range of options established by the company's authorized financial institution. And if the performance of one option is better than that of another option, you can move your money around.

■ Many 401(k) plans allow you to withdraw funds for hardship reasons before you reach the age of 59½. (That's the age you must be in ordinary circumstances to begin withdrawing money from your 401(k) without paying a

10 percent penalty tax.) Legislation has recently expanded the situations that allow for withdrawal of funds without penalty.

■ If you leave the company you work for, you can take your 401(k) funds with you and roll them over into another retirement plan without paying taxes or a penalty for withdrawing funds.

When you participate in a 401(k) program, you receive an earnings statement every quarter. You'll be pleased to see your savings grow. You're also able to compare the various funds in which you have invested. Based on these comparisons, you may want to make changes in the allocation of your funds when the opportunity to do so arrives.

Ten Tips for Saving Money

The following tips can help you save the money you need to make your financial goals become realities. Remember that if you don't save, you won't be able to afford the things you want, and you won't have a secure financial future.

Set up a separate savings account

Establishing a separate account for your savings is important because doing so enables you to watch your savings grow and see milestones. Don't let your savings "mingle" with your regular checking account because spending it would be too easy. If you keep your savings separate, it is more secure. You also earn a greater rate of interest on your savings account than you would if you left the money in your checking account.

A separate savings account may help you avoid monthly charges on your checking account. Many banks waive the monthly checking fee if you also have a savings account with them.

The first bill you pay out of your paycheck — whether you actually write a check or you have the amount automatically deducted — should be the savings amount you're committed to living without.

Learn to live on less

Take another look at your net income (see Chapter 3). Whatever it is, reduce it (on paper!) by 10 percent. Then take that 90 percent figure as the amount you have to work with for your personal budget. What do you do with the 10 percent that you "no longer have"? Put it in your savings account.

If taking 10 percent off your net income seems too drastic, then try this approach: When you next sit down to review your budget and pay your bills, write a check for 1 percent of your take-home pay and deposit it in your separate savings account. The second month, take 2 percent off the top of your take-home pay and put it in savings. Increase the amount by 1 percent each month. By the end of one year, you'll be saving 12 percent of your net income.

Use automatic deductions for savings

If having your savings tied to your net paycheck is too "dangerous" because you just may wind up spending what you indented to save, then arrange for automatic deductions. For example, you can have as little as $50 taken from each paycheck and transferred automatically to your savings account or money market account. You can also have money automatically deducted and put into a 401(k) account or other type of investment.

Avoid credit cards

Leave your credit cards behind. Impulse purchases are tempting when you carry plastic. These impulse buys add up, and they basically destroy your budget and erode your commitment to responsible money management.

When you pay by cash or check, you significantly reduce the amount you spend. As an added benefit, you avoid the outrageous credit card interest rates that compound in the blink of an eye.

Limit yourself to one credit card, or use the two-card system described in Chapter 5. In any case, avoid using them. Consider the card as an emergency backup, not a constant companion. Don't be lulled into thinking that you need a credit card to establish your credit rating; you don't.

Reduce your taxes

Contributing to a 401(k) plan may reduce your take-home pay, but it also reduces your tax liability. In other words, you are taxed based on the money remaining after your investments or contributions are deducted from your gross income. Other qualified retirement plans do the same. If you invest in an IRA or Keogh, you can also defer your tax liability. Other investments that are tax-free or partially exempt include municipal bonds, EE Savings Bonds, and U.S. Treasury Bills.

An *Individual Retirement Account (IRA)* is a private retirement plan that allows individuals or married couples to save a certain amount of their income every year, depending on their income(s). Contributions to a traditional IRA are not taxed, and the interest is tax-deferred. (Contributions to a Roth IRA are made after taxes are taken out, so these IRAs do not reduce taxable income.)

A *Keogh plan* is another type of retirement account that allows self-employed persons to save a maximum of 20 percent of their income and deduct their contributions from their annual taxable income.

Municipal bonds are fixed-income securities issued by government agencies to support general state or local government needs or special projects. These securities are exempt from federal and most state and local income taxes if they are issued in the state in which you live.

EE Savings Bonds are U.S. government-issued savings instruments in values ranging from $50 to $10,000. They are purchased at a discount and redeemed at face value at maturity. From 1941 to 1979, the government issued series E bonds. After 1979, the federal government issued EE Savings Bonds.

U.S. Treasury Bills (T-Bills) are issued by Federal Reserve banks for the U.S. Treasury as a means of borrowing money for short periods. The bills are sold at a discount and are redeemed at face value at maturity (up to one year). Because the federal government issues T-Bills, they are free of default risk and assumed to be the safest form of investment.

Homeowners enjoy additional tax benefits. For example, they can deduct real estate taxes and the interest they have paid on mortgage loans from their taxable income. Charitable donations also reduce taxable income.

The IRS has many free publications that can help you reduce your taxes — call 800-829-3676 to order them.

Save all "found" money

Consider all "found" or extra money as direct contributions to your savings plan. Found money can consist of monetary gifts, dividends, or interest income. Without delay, deposit this money in your special savings account and smile. Don't let yourself feel deprived that you're being denied a splurge. Instead, concentrate on the fact that you'll have the pleasure of seeing a long-range goal come true. A small, immediate pleasure is a small price to pay for a greater sense of accomplishment.

The longer you let gift money sit around at home, the less likely it is that you'll save it.

After you pay a debt, save the same amount

What a great sense of relief you get when you pay off your car, your student loans, or an installment loan! When you finish writing that last check, put down your pen and smile. But next month, when you go to pay your bills, write a check for the same amount (or even half the amount) and put it into your special savings account.

Remember that you learned to live with that debt as part of your fixed expenses. After the loan or debt is paid off, you can continue to do without that money.

Do your research

Most libraries have a good collection of books and materials on personal finances. Many also engage speakers who are experts in various aspects of finance and investing. Lots of people have good ideas about saving money. You can benefit from their experience and suggestions. (See the CliffsNotes Resource Center at the back of this book for recommended titles.)

Even if you walk away with only one good idea per book, that idea will keep you growing as a money manager. And once you have accumulated some money in your savings account, you'll want direction about investing your hard-saved money. (See also Chapter 7 for information about investing.)

Use a piggy bank

When you were a child, you may have been encouraged to make contributions to a piggy bank. Get a "piggy bank" for yourself now. A large jar, or something you can see through, is best. At the end of every day, empty the change from your wallet or pants pocket and put it in the piggy bank. Next to the piggy bank, keep a notebook; in it, record the amount of change you put into the bank. At the end of every week, tally the amount that you have contributed to the piggy bank.

If you can, set up a matching strategy for your piggy bank savings. When you tally the week's collection at the end of the week, add the same amount all at once to the jar. You can double your savings in a pretty painless way. You can plan to take this money to the bank when your piggy bank is full to the brim or on a special occasion, whatever suits your personality.

Set up a money-saver buddy system

Saving money doesn't have to feel like drudgery, and it doesn't have to make you a miser. A little motivation from a friend can help. Think about finding a money buddy to help you save money regularly. Your money buddy can be someone from work, a relative, or a neighbor whom you know, or suspect, is also trying to save money.

Invite your money buddy to share a sack lunch with you one day a week, or if lunch isn't convenient, make it a phone call. Compare notes on your progress and offer each other encouragement. Swap ideas for saving money that you may have come across in an article or a conversation.

Building a Nest Egg for the Future

I love those tables that show you how much time it takes for savings to grow. For example, if you save $72 a week at 8 percent interest, in one year you will have $3,900. In five years, you will have $23,000. In 30 years, you will have $468,000. The growth may seem like magic, but it isn't.

A nest egg starts out small. But if you don't start it, it won't grow. The following sections give you a look at some savings mileposts. See what it takes to arrive at each milepost, and think about what you can do when you get there.

Step 1: Save $100

Your first goal is to save $100. You may be in a position simply to write a check for $100 and say, "There, it's done!" But saving $100 may take you some time and effort. Use Table 6-1 to be specific about how long it will take you to save $100 and how you will do it. If you need to, break up the goal into mini goals so that you can work your way toward the $100 total.

Table 6-1:   Saving $100

Goal	Target Date	Strategies
Save $100		

The time to start saving that $100 is now. Do *something,* even if you simply put $1 in an envelope. Then you know that you've begun.

Think of the things that you might want to do with the $100 you save. The options are awesome. You might be tempted to splurge and throw a party. You might use it to pay off a debt. You might use it to begin an investment plan. I'll save the investing options for Chapter 7, where I examine investment strategies for that $100.

Step 2: Save $1,000

Chapter 3 suggests that you can save $1,000 a year simply by finding a way to reduce your spending by $2.74 a day. There are others ways to save that $1,000, too. You can do whatever you did to save $100 ten times. But you may have a different time frame in mind.

Use Table 6-2 to be specific about when and how you will save $1,000. Challenge yourself to think of ways to save $1,000 in one year. Again, if you need to, break up the big goal of saving $1,000 into smaller, more easily attainable goals.

Table 6-2:   Saving $1,000

Goal	Estimated Time	Strategies
Save $1,000		

When you meet this goal, you've saved some serious money. If you're debt-free, perhaps you can start thinking about a down payment for a home, or a degree, or another investment strategy (see Chapter 7).

Step 3: Save $10,000

Before you moan and think, "There's no way I'll ever have $10,000 saved," pause and think about the kind of life you will be living if you don't save $10,000. No matter what your circumstances are, you have the power and the ability to achieve this goal.

You're probably not going to be able to save $10,000 within one year. Here's where your dedication and endurance training will serve you well. You must stay motivated with a clear goal. Keep the prize in mind. What will you do with that $10,000? The possibilities are endless.

Use Table 6-3 to realistically assess how you'll save $10,000 and how long it will take. Remember that if you save $72 a week with 8 percent interest, you'll have $3,900 in one year. In three years, you'll have $12,700. You'll be ahead of your goal of saving $10,000 in less than three years. Fill in your own mini-goals in the blanks in the first column, and then include a time frame and strategy for each mini-goal.

Table 6-3: Saving $10,000

Goal	Estimated Time	Strategies
Save $10,000		

Give yourself a pat on the back for realizing that it just might be possible to commit to a savings plan that will bring you $10,000.

The amount you have saved is your entrance fee to the world of investing. And the investment world is where your money will grow over time to give you greater financial security.

CHAPTER 7
CREATING AN INVESTING PLAN

IN THIS CHAPTER

- ■ Knowing how to put your money to work for you and contribute to your financial security

- ■ Remembering that most investments start out small

- ■ Learning to make wise investments

Face it: Very few people achieve financial security by inheriting a lot of money, winning the lottery, or marrying a very rich person. If you look around, however, you'll find many financially secure people. How do they do it? The answer is probably *investing*.

You're ready to make the move from saver to investor when you're free of credit card debt and other major obligations, and after you've saved for an emergency fund. That emergency fund covers six to nine months of expenses in case you're laid off or without work.

You can become an investor when you also meet the following conditions:

- ■ You have your financial goals clearly in mind.

- ■ You're able to distinguish your economic needs from your wants, and you have the discipline to postpone or alter your choices if you need to.

- ■ You can stick to a budget and spend less than you earn.

- ■ You save what you don't spend.

If you're on board with these conditions, this chapter takes a look at your investment options. Although there are no guarantees in the world of investing, there are some guidelines that you should follow.

Avoiding the Roller-Coaster Approach

You've probably heard the horror stories and triumphant tales of investing. Somebody just made millions by following a hot tip overheard on the golf course. Somebody else just lost everything when she borrowed a bundle to invest in real estate in Florida.

You want to avoid the roller-coaster approach to investing. Roller coasters belong in amusement parks. Good, steady growth over the long haul is your goal for investing.

Getting Free Investing Practice by Doing a Rehearsal

To learn some investment strategies *before* you get out your checkbook, give yourself $5,000 in play money. Start a notebook to track your "rehearsal" investments.

Many options clamor for your investment dollars. As in marriage, it's best to get to know the candidates before making a choice too quickly and regretting it later. Take a look at the summary of common investment options in Table 7-1.

Table 7-1: Common Investment Options

Type of Investment	Comments
Interest Investments	
Savings accounts	Safe, but low interest rates.

Continued

Table 7-1: *continued*

Type of Investment	Comments
Interest Investments	
Money market funds	Better rates than you would earn from a simple savings account, but minimum balances required. Considered safe.
Certificates of Deposit (CDs)	Bank rates vary, so shop around. FDIC-insured up to $100,000.
Municipal bonds	Guaranteed tax-free returns, but low interest rates. Rated in terms of risk and vary in safety.
Treasury securities	Rates vary, with some attractive; secure and considered very safe because they're backed by the federal government.
Bond funds	A variety of bond options managed by a professional investor; diversified bond holdings help minimize risk.
Stocks	
U.S. common stock	Historically popular; hold for the long run
Preferred stock	Good dividend income
Mutual funds	A variety of stocks managed by a professional investor
Initial public offerings (IPOs)	First-time sale of a company's stock; high risk!
Foreign stocks	Growth may be unstable; can hedge with international global mutual funds
Real Estate	
Home	Appreciation over the long run
Rental property	Being a landlord has its headaches

Note: Investment opportunities such as stock options, commodity futures, precious metals, junk bonds, and financial derivatives are omitted from this list. In the opinion of many veteran investors, these investments are not good choices for beginners, so walk away from them for now.

Tip

Now, with your practice $5,000, you must make a basic decision: Will you invest it all in one place or *diversify* (by investing in a variety of stocks, bonds, or and mutual funds)? Most experts claim that diversifying your investments is a good strategy.

For the sake of gaining practice, fill out Table 7-2. Be sure to note the level of risk associated with each option. Use this table to help you identify what you expect from your $5,000 investment and when. This worksheet can also help you identify the investment options that will work best for your goals.

You can find information about current interest rates, or *rates of return,* in your local newspaper and in financial magazines. These rates will vary, as will your perception of risk. Do your best to fill out the table with realistic information and be honest with yourself in evaluating your perception of risk. You might give a 5 to the kind of investment with the most risk and 1 to the least risky investments.

Table 7-2:   My Investment Possibilities

Option	Risk	Expected 1-Year Rate of Return	Expected 5-Year Rate of Return
Savings account			
Money market account			
Stocks			
Mutual funds			
CDs			
Municipal bonds			
Bond mutual funds			
Real estate			
Other			

Tip

Ask yourself what level of risk you're comfortable with in your investments. Most investors select some "safe" investments, such as CDs, and some riskier options as well. Decide what percentage of the $5,000 you want in a "safe" investment and what amount you're willing to invest in a riskier option.

For the sake of your rehearsal, assume that you want to invest in a CD, a mutual fund, and a municipal bond. These investments will give you a pretty safe and predictable return on your $5,000 investment.

CDs: Safe investments

A *certificate of deposit* is an interest-bearing time deposit issued by a bank. You loan your money to the bank, and the bank promises a guaranteed rate of interest that is higher than regular savings, over a specified period of time, ranging for 30 days to 10 years.

The advantages of investing in CDs include

- The deposit is FDIC-insured up to $100,000.

- The fixed rate of interest is greater than the interest accrued in regular savings accounts.

- You can select a duration for the deposit to suit your short-term or long-term needs. (Remember that there are substantial penalties for withdrawing money early!)

Say you want to invest $1,000 in a short-term CD. Do some comparison shopping for CD interest rates. Your comparison-shopping can involve looking at the published rates in the daily *The New York Times* and *The Wall Street Journal,* reading bank advertising about CDs in your local paper, going to www.rate.net, www.bankcd.com, or www.money-rates.com on the Internet to get CD rates, or making a trip or call to your local bank(s).

Now make your best rehearsal choice for a CD. In your notebook, write down what the rate of return is and when that CD is due.

Mutual funds: Diversified, managed stocks

When you're new to investing, a mutual fund enables you to get your feet wet and diversify your holdings without taking on a great deal of risk. Say you want to invest $2,000 of your "rehearsal" money in a mutual fund. With your investment, you become part owner of a variety of stocks. But individual stock ownership in the mutual fund is not important; the performance of the fund as a whole is what counts. When you invest in a mutual fund, you are basically buying skilled management of funds, not individual stocks.

Mutual funds come in two types:

- **Load fund:** You purchase a load fund through a broker who charges a commission. You can pay the commission up front with the initial investment or at the back end when you exit the fund.

- **No-load fund:** You buy a no-load fund directly from the company, and there are no sales charges or commissions.

You may think that the obvious better choice is a no-load fund, but in some cases, the skill of the mutual fund's managers is worth the commission because you get better returns.

Investing in a mutual fund has plenty of advantages. For example:

- You achieve diversification with each share you buy in a mutual fund. Each share is used to buy a range of stocks.

■ You avoid wild price fluctuations that an individual stock might experience.

■ You can sell back your shares in the mutual fund at any time, hopefully at a profit, giving you maximum liquidity (the ability to convert your investment into cash).

■ You can automatically reinvest your dividends so that your account keeps growing without your having to pay additional commissions and taxes.

Now comes the hard part — choosing a mutual fund. Thousands of mutual funds are on the market today. How do you sort it all out? Try starting in the newspaper. If your local paper doesn't carry weekly information about the performance of mutual funds, pay a visit to your local library. You can also try Morningstar or a paper like *Investors Business Daily* or *The Wall Street Journal*.

Most Sunday papers carry expanded financial information. My paper carries a section that summarizes the performance of several mutual funds in each of three categories — those with higher-than-average risk, average risk, and lower-than-average risk. Compare the returns for funds in each category and select the type of mutual fund that best suits your investment strategy.

Before you invest money in a mutual fund, get information about the fund. Do your research at the library or on the Internet, or write or call the company for a copy of its annual report and prospectus. A company issues an *annual report,* which indicates the performance of the corporation over the past year. A *prospectus* is a publication that describes the security or stock being offered for sale to the public. It includes disclosures regarding risk, financial statements, management structure, and business objectives.

For the "rehearsal," imagine investing $2,000 in each of three different funds so that you can compare performance. In your investment notebook, keep a separate page for each mutual fund and record the following as column headings: name of mutual fund, date of your "rehearsal" purchase, cost per share, number of shares purchased, and date/amount of change.

Every week, review the value of each mutual fund you "invested" in. Track the numbers in your investment notebook for three months, and then compare your three funds. Based on performance, which mutual fund would you choose to invest in for real? (You may also want to look at the longer-term performance of your funds, which you can find on Morningstar.)

Municipal bonds: Tax-free investments

Cities, counties, states, and special agencies issue municipal bonds to finance various projects. Many investors call these bonds "munis." The biggest advantage is that the interest paid on munis is exempt from federal income tax. As an extra bonus, if you're a resident of the state or city issuing the muni, your earnings are also exempt from state and local taxes. This is known as a *double tax-free bond.*

That's the good news. The downside of municipal bonds is that they often require a substantial minimum investment. In some cases, the minimum investment is $5,000 (there goes your whole bundle!), but in other instances, you can buy munis for a minimum of $1,000. Shop around. You may have to go to a broker or bank to buy a muni bond.

Bonds receive a rating from Moody and Standard & Poors (S&P). Ratings range from AAA, for the best quality, to D, meaning that the bond issue is in default. Any bond rated Ba (Moody) or BB (S&P) or lower is risky and should be avoided.

Select a municipal bond or a municipal bond fund for your "rehearsal" and record your purchase price and date in your investment notebook. Make a chart to track the performance of your virtual investment over a fiscal quarter at the very least.

Track the performance of your "investments" over a period of at least three months. Then study your investment returns. What did better than you expected? What did worse? What adjustments would you make to your "investment portfolio"? Your analysis of the rehearsal performance can guide your selection of actual investment options.

Managing Your Investments

If you went through the investing rehearsal, you now have a sense of the amount of information you need to make wise investments. The front end of investing involves research, which takes time and effort. But there's more to investing than just making choices based on your research and good judgment. A lot of record keeping and evaluation go on, as well. This stage is where you can sharpen your skills as a money manager.

You can continue to "rehearse" your investment strategies until you actually accomplish your savings goal. Remember that you can begin investing with a very small sum of money. The important thing is to start now!

Watching your money grow

After you make your first investment, you want to see it grow quickly. Table 7-3 shows you how quickly your money would grow if you invested $2,000 a year, assuming an annual growth rate of 8 percent and continued investment until age 65.

Table 7-3: Growth of Investment

Starting at Age	Total Actually Saved	Total Value at Age 65
19	$92,000	$837,000
27	$76,000	$441,000
37	$56,000	$191,000
47	$36,000	$75,000

The conclusion is obvious: The sooner you start saving and investing, the more money you'll have for retirement.

Using the Rule of 72

A quick way to calculate how long it will take an investment to double — at any interest rate — is to use the Rule of 72. Simply divide 72 by the interest rate, and you have the number of years it will take for your investment to double. For example, if you have an investment earning 8 percent, divide 72 by 8 percent to find that it will take nine years for your investment to double in value.

Just think: If you made an initial investment of $10,000 when your child was born and earned 8 percent interest on that investment, that child would have $40,000 at age 18. That money could help pay for a college education!

Keeping track of your investments

Whether your investments are virtual, as in the rehearsal exercise, or real, as they will be once you save that first $100 or $1,000, you need to keep track of essential information and make regular evaluations. In addition to the half-hour a week that you spend developing your money-management skills, add half an hour a month for keeping your investment record in order.

I suggest starting an investment notebook. This notebook doesn't have to be fancy. But organize it so that it includes essential information about each investment, and leave room to grow as your information expands.

Some investors find that a three-ring binder is a better way to organize investment information. Dividers quickly identify each particular investment. You might include your monthly budget worksheets in the binder as well. In addition, you can add a section for your credit cards to keep track of that important information.

Table 7-4 shows a sample investment notebook page. This worksheet can help you organize your records and reduce your frustration when you can't find an important document or phone number. Make multiple copies of this sheet for your investment notebook, or create your own sheets.

Table 7-4:   Sample Investment Notebook Page

Name of investment
Common abbreviation
Name of broker or exchange
Address
Phone
Fax
E-mail
Account number
Date of purchase
Amount of initial investment
Price per share/unit
Number of initial shares/units

Then track the investment's value, change in value, and activity (did you sell or buy shares, for example?), and record any comments you have about the investment.

CHAPTER 8

MAKING YOUR BANK WORK FOR YOU

IN THIS CHAPTER

- Taking advantage of a personal banker
- Setting up saving and checking accounts
- Reconciling your accounts

Banking services are a fact of your financial life, so you want to make banking a useful (and pleasant) experience. Just as you would "shop around" before you made a major purchase, so should you do some comparison shopping before making a commitment to a particular bank. Look for convenience and personal service in addition to good rates. Your bank will become your assistant as you gain experience in taking control of your money.

Looking at Bank Services

From the array of available banks — commercial, industrial, independent, and state — you want a bank that is convenient and that provides the services that are important to *you*.

 Look for a bank that federally insures your deposits. The Federal Deposit Insurance Corporation (FDIC), the Savings Association Insurance Fund (SAIF), and the National Credit Union Association (NCUA) insure the majority of savings account deposits — usually up to $100,000.

For most people, a bank provides two basic services: checking accounts and savings accounts. But you can also use a bank to purchase certificates of deposit, to open a money market account, to obtain a loan for a car or college tuition, or to buy a home. Of course, the bank often charges for each of the services you use. In fact, you may have to pay about $200 a year in bank charges if you don't compare bank costs. As a smart money manager, you want to shop around.

Following are charges that a bank may enforce:

- A service charge if you don't maintain a minimum balance in your checking and/or savings accounts (***Note:*** Some banks link your checking and savings accounts to make meeting the minimum requirement easier.)

- A service charge for each check returned due to insufficient funds

- A service charge for printing your checks

You can save up to 50 percent by ordering your checks directly from outside providers. Note, however, that there have been instances of fraud with some check providers.

- A service charge for visiting the automated teller machine (ATM) or a human teller

- A per-check charge for each check you write

Almost all banks offer the same basic services to their customers; the thing that sets one bank apart from another is its personal service. A personal banker helps you with all the services your bank offers, helps you solve any problems that may arise, and facilitates and "personalizes" the services you want from a bank.

If this type of personal service is important to you, seek it out and don't settle for less.

Starting a Bank Account

When starting with a new bank, I recommend that you open a checking account and a separate savings account (see Chapter 6). Be prepared to make several decisions at this time, because the bank will offer you a variety of choices (which I discuss later in the chapter).

After selecting a bank, you can walk in and open your accounts, or better yet, you can call first and schedule an appointment with a personal banker. When you call, ask what you need to bring with you to open your account(s). Your personal banker will probably tell you to bring four things: money to open an account, your social security number, a driver's license or passport, and the mailing address to which you want your bank statements sent.

During your appointment with the personal banker, give yourself plenty of time to open your accounts and ask your questions. You don't want to seem in a rush because you may not receive all the information and attention that the banker can give you. Conclude your interview by asking whether you can contact the personal banker with questions or when you need assistance. Shake hands on the response and make a point to call your banker within a week to say thanks for the assistance.

Checking Accounts

Several kinds of checking accounts are available. You need to select the one that works best for you.

Regular checking accounts

A regular checking account is the most basic. With such an account, you can write any number of checks, and you may not have to maintain a minimum balance. However, the money you have in your checking account doesn't earn interest, and the bank usually charges a monthly service fee.

A few banks offer free checking — sometimes only if you maintain a minimum balance. If you decide to start such an account, know what the minimum balance is and how much you'll be charged if your balance falls below that amount.

NOW accounts

Most banks offer some version of a NOW (Negotiable Order of Withdrawal) account. NOW accounts require that you keep a minimum balance in your checking account. You may not earn much interest, but you do avoid monthly service charges.

Banks generally expect you to maintain a $500 minimum balance in a NOW account. If you choose this type of account, just pretend that $500 doesn't exist. You can even "hide it" in your check register by deducting it from the amount you show in your account.

In the long run, a minimum-balance type of account is usually cheaper than one with a monthly service fee.

Special checking accounts

Some banks offer special arrangements for targeted customers:

- **Super-NOW accounts:** These accounts are available for customers who can afford to leave greater minimum balances in their checking accounts. For example, if a customer can leave $2,500 as a minimum balance in the checking account, then the bank waives the monthly service charge and agrees to pay a modest rate of interest on the amount in the account. In addition, most Super-NOW accounts provide overdraft protection.

With *overdraft protection,* when you have insufficient funds in your checking account to cover the amount of a check you've written, the bank pays the check for you and then usually automatically transfers money from your savings account or credit line into your checking account to cover that amount.

- **Free checking accounts:** Because senior citizens typically represent a safe and stable segment of the population, banks often offer them free checking accounts in the hope of getting additional business.

Remember

A free checking account means that no monthly service charge and individual check fee is charged the customer, but a minimum balance may be required.

- **Money market accounts:** This type of account also allows you to write checks. The bank pays a higher rate of interest on funds in this kind of account, but the monthly number of free checks is very limited — usually three. After that, you pay a steep service charge per check.

Savings Accounts

Setting up and building a savings account is important if you want to be able to make the investments that can help you achieve financial security. In Chapter 3, I advise you to consider savings as one of your fixed expenses because building a savings account is the first step toward accumulating money for investing, vacations, and so on.

Following are a few benefits you get from having a savings account:

- **You receive interest on your money.** The bank's interest rates on savings accounts vary; in general, they're low.

■ **You have ready access to your funds (called *liquidity*).** You can withdraw the money in your savings account at any time without penalty.

■ **Your funds are safe.** When you bank with an FDIC bank, your money is insured up to $100,000. (After that, you need to find another investment strategy and/or open a second account!)

To make the most of savings with the least amount of effort, first take advantage of direct deposit, if your company offers you that option. With direct deposit, you don't have to wait for your paycheck to reach the bank, worry about its being lost in the mail, or drive to the bank to deposit it yourself.

After you make arrangements to automatically deposit your paycheck (or even if you still deposit the check yourself) set up an automatic transfer of money into your savings account. Refer to your budget to find out how much you can set aside for savings from each paycheck (see Chapter 3). Then arrange to have that amount transferred into your savings account with each paycheck.

Finally, don't forget the extra deposits. Simply take any additional money that you can add to your savings account to the bank and fill out a deposit slip. Reward yourself for those "extra" deposits. The rewards don't have to cost money. Call a friend. Walk around the block. Do something good for yourself!

Electronic and ATM Banking

Every bank has a fancy brochure to identify the services it offers and explain its electronic and ATM systems. The ATM is the most popular type of electronic banking that customers use. Most people enjoy the convenience and flexibility that ATMs and other forms of electronic banking offer.

Electronic services

You can access your account information and bank services through your telephone or computer. When you bank by a Touch-Tone phone, you can obtain your checking account and savings account balances; your deposit and withdrawal activity for the past month or more; the status of specific checks — paid or outstanding — charged to your account; current interest rate information; and the location and hours of each bank with its branches. You can also transfer money between your checking and savings accounts, make payments on loans, mortgages, or bank credit cards, and obtain credit advances.

Many banks provide a toll-free number that you can use to make telephone transactions. Some offer a practice line to demonstrate how telephone banking works, which eliminates the anxiety connected with first-time use and helps you short-cut the menu of options when you actually perform a transaction via telephone.

Many banks also provide online access to their information and services. Several have partnered with money management software programs to help you manage your accounts through your personal computer. In addition to providing the same information and services as telephone banking, online customers can actually work on their budgets, generate financial reports, and pay bills without writing checks.

Many good software programs are also available to help you track and manage your money and put together your personal budget. When you use such a software program, you will find that record keeping and account management becomes much easier to deal with. See Chapter 10 for suggestions about getting and staying organized financially.

ATM banking

ATM (automated teller machine) transactions let you get account information and perform transactions at many convenient locations throughout your city and the world. The most common use for an ATM card is to withdraw money from your checking or savings account. But you can use your ATM card for other things as well:

- Make deposits to your checking or savings account

- Obtain a mini statement of recent transactions with current account balance (***Note:*** Some banks charge additional fees for these ATM services)

- Make payments on bank loans

Remember that the easier it is to withdraw money, the more often you're tempted to do it. Frequent ATM stops can jeopardize your budget and savings plan. You also often pay a service charge for using an ATM card. Investigate the fees and the "free" locations you're likely to use before you start banking this way. Finally, ATM locations are available for use 24 hours a day, so follow commonsense safety precautions.

Your telephone and ATM transactions are protected by a password. After you select your password, commit it to memory and store the original PIN (Personal Identification Number) statement in a safe place like a bank safety deposit box.

Dealing with Bank Statements

After you set up your checking and savings accounts, you receive monthly bank statements. With a bank statement, you can track your bills and, if you use a bank credit card, your spending. You can also compare deposits and withdrawals and learn how much interest is working for you.

Reconciling your checking account

The night or weekend after your bank statement arrives is a good time to reserve for your routine review and "reconciliation" of your checkbook. The goal is to review your deposits and withdrawals over the past month and note any discrepancies between your records and the bank's.

The process is not hard or even lengthy. Just follow these steps:

1. Find the ending balance for your checking account on the bank statement and compare the bank figure with the figure in your check register.

   Check the dates carefully. Some of the transactions that you have recorded may not have cleared with the bank yet. Do not include these transactions in your calculations.

Remember

2. If you see a significant difference (more than $20), check your arithmetic with a calculator. If math error doesn't account for the discrepancy, then write the bank figure in your register and proceed with Step 3. You will have to return to the discrepancy after the current month's reconciliation.

3. Check off each check paid by the bank both in your register and on your statement. If you find a gap in the number sequence, look to see whether that check was paid previously or is still outstanding.

4. Use the calculator to add up the amount of all your checks paid out that month. That number should be the same as the total figure identified for checks by your bank.

5. Examine all the electronic withdrawals that you've made with your ATM card and/or your bank card; then add these up on your calculator.

6. Check for transactions that you have forgotten to record — for example, service fees. Record any missing information in your check register.

7. Combine the total amount of your checks with the total amount of your electronic withdrawals and other fees. This final amount should equal the figure identified as the total withdrawals made for the month.

The most common source of discrepancy between your records and the bank statement is arithmetic. You may want to use a calculator to check your additions and subtractions. The second most common source is forgetting to record a transaction — either a deposit or a withdrawal.

After you reconcile your bank statement to your own records as reported in your check register, pat yourself on the back. If your starting balance as calculated in your check register was significantly different from the figure identified by the bank, however, you still have work to do. Back up month by month until you find the error.

If, despite your best efforts and conscientious record-keeping, you can't reconcile your records with the bank statement, give your personal banker a call and make an appointment to go over the records. Ask about additional charges for reviewing your statements — some banks charge for this service.

Following are a couple things to keep in mind as you reconcile your checking account:

■ Many bank statements break down banking activity day by day, which can be useful as you try to identify trends in your spending habits or when you need to track down a mistake or a forgotten purchase.

■ If you have a linked savings account, the bank statement will show any activity in terms of deposits and withdrawals. It will also identify the total amount of money in the savings account and the amount of interest paid in the statement period and year-to-date.

Many people like using commercial money management software like Quicken or Microsoft Money to help them track this information.

Handling mistakes

Chances are that someday you'll find a mistake in your records or your bank statements. To prevent or remedy mistakes, do the following:

■ When you make a deposit or withdrawal, check the receipt for accurate amounts and account numbers *before* you leave the bank.

■ Check your bank statements when they come to identify mistakes as soon as possible.

■ Keep accurate records of your transactions so that you can prove a deposit or a withdrawal.

■ After a mistake is corrected, ask the bank how the correction will be reported on your financial records. You don't want a late payment to show up on your credit rating if it didn't happen.

CHAPTER 9
PLANNING FOR THE INEVITABLE: TAXES

IN THIS CHAPTER

- Understanding federal and state income taxes
- Being aware of "hidden" taxes
- Amassing and organizing your tax records
- Staying out of tax trouble

When I used to complain about the amount of income tax I had to pay, my mother would say, "Just be glad you have the money to pay it." So I tried to adjust my attitude. I still resent the amount of taxes I pay, but I'm grateful that I have the money to pay what I have to.

Some taxes are paid out every day. For states with a sales tax, you pay a sales tax on every purchase you make. The gasoline you buy at $1.239 a gallon covers up taxes added on by the federal, state, and county in which you buy the gas. You don't see the breakdown for each taxing agency, so you don't notice the taxes as easily.

Federal Income Taxes

Federal income taxes have become so complex that most Americans need help figuring out what they owe and how to report their income. Ignorance only compounds tax problems. You can't claim that you don't know the tax requirements and expect your tax debt to be forgiven.

Staying informed

Tip

Purchase a tax preparation guide every year. These guides keep you informed and are tax-deductible. Even if you choose to have a professional prepare your taxes, the current tax guide enables you to ask informed questions.

Table 9-1 is a partial list of free publications available from the IRS. If any of the publications seems useful to you, order it by calling 800-829-3676. (Your local library and bookstore have additional titles and software that can help you get information about your taxes.)

Table 9-1:   Free Publications from the IRS

Publication Number	Title
1	Your Rights As a Taxpayer
17	Your Federal Income Tax*
334	Tax Guide for Small Businesses
504	Tax Information for Divorced or Separated Individuals
525	Taxable and Nontaxable Income
530	Tax Information for Homeowners
552	Recordkeeping for Individuals and a List of Tax Publications
553	Tax Information for Older Americans
910	Guide to Free Tax Services

*Especially recommended for its concrete information and suggestions.

Getting organized

Whether you do your taxes yourself or you turn the task over to a professional, you need the proper records. More than half the time spent on preparing income taxes is related to keeping and organizing records and studying the rules and procedures for filing. If you keep good records, you have completed more than half the battle!

Set up a separate file drawer or box that can accommodate folders. At the beginning of each calendar year, buy manila folders and label them with the year and any of the following categories that apply to your situation. (No matter what time of year you're reading this, organize your folders for the current year *now.*) Then save your receipts and other information in the appropriate folders.

- **W-2 forms:** Your employer is required to send you income information in January of each year. Your *W-2 form* tells you and the IRS how much money you earned and how much tax was withheld.

- **1099 forms:** These forms report money you receive from freelance assignments, interest payments from banks, and stock dividends.

- **Alimony:** Alimony is the amount paid to a former spouse under a divorce or separation agreement. You're allowed to deduct the money you pay for alimony from your gross income. You report alimony payments that you receive as income.

- **IRA:** A traditional Individual Retirement Account (IRA) is a personal savings account that you set aside for retirement by using pretax dollars. (Roth IRAs also exist, but these accounts use after-tax dollars.) You can subtract the amount you contribute to a traditional IRA from your taxable income.

- **Deductions — Medical:** You can deduct medical and dental expenses that exceed 7.5 percent of your adjusted gross income.

- **Deductions — Taxes:** You can deduct your state income taxes (and any local or foreign income taxes) when you itemize your deductions. In addition, you can deduct real estate taxes.

- **Deductions — Interest:** You can deduct some interest payments from your tax liability. Most home mortgages and home equity loans are tax-deductible.

Interest on personal loans, credit charges, and car loans are not tax deductible.

- **Deductions — Charity:** You can deduct from your income tax contributions that you made to charitable and not-for-profit organizations. Some limitations apply, but save your receipts.

- **Moving expenses:** Many expenses connected with changes in the location of your employment can reduce your gross income if you move further than 50 miles.

- **Home expenses:** Save all records and receipts connected with buying or improving your home. These records become the basis for calculating your capital loss or gain when you sell your home.

- **Deductions — Work:** The cost of certain tools, uniforms, memberships, training programs, mileage, and books can be tax-deductible if they're related to improvement and on-the-job training.

- **Deductions — Travel and Entertainment:** Travel expenses require special record keeping. Usually, business-related deductions for travel and entertainment have a 50 percent limitation.

Deciding whether to itemize

Whether or not you do your own taxes, you have to decide whether claiming the standard deduction or itemizing your deductions will work better for you.

A tax adviser can review your tax situation and recommend whether itemizing your deductions would be more beneficial. Generally, if your tax situation is fairly simple, claiming the standard deduction is easier. If, however, you have had outstanding medical expenses, have purchased a home, or have made some other significant change in your life, then itemizing deductions may be in your best interest.

If the total value of your itemized deductions exceeds the value of the standardized deduction, it's better to itemize your deductions and file the more detailed tax return. Take the time to complete the tax worksheets found in tax guidebooks and software, which can help you decide whether to itemize.

State Income Taxes

Most states impose an income tax for the "privilege" of earning or receiving income there. Individuals, as well as corporations, trusts, and estates, are taxed to generate revenue for the state. Only seven states don't tax personal income: Alaska, Florida, Nevada, South Dakota, Texas, Washington, and Wyoming. New Hampshire and Tennessee tax only interest and dividend income. The states that don't have income taxes finance expenditures largely through sales or property taxes.

Understanding how state governments impose income tax

States have more variety in their taxing procedures than the federal government does. Conditions vary from state to state, and you need to know your state's requirements. In general, the rates for the state income taxes are much lower than the rates for federal income taxes. States also prepare tax information to assist taxpayers with completing their forms. Both state and federal information is commonly available at post offices, libraries, and other locations.

Getting the records you need

You use the same records to complete your state and federal forms. See the section "Getting organized" for a list of these items. You file state income taxes simultaneously with your federal forms. Figures for adjusted gross income relate to the deductions for federal and state taxes. You receive state forms in the mail, or you can pick them up at post offices, public libraries, and tax preparation offices.

Other Taxes

States have been searching for ways to generate additional revenues to finance their many programs and services. After the Great Depression, many states came up with the idea of adding a sales tax to the retail sale of goods and services to help finance new programs. Over the years, additional taxes have been added, some hidden and some obvious. Only when you know what's being taxed can you take steps to legally reduce the amount of taxes you pay.

Knowing what gets taxed

States, counties, and municipalities have the right to secure funding through taxation. And they're very good at identifying additional sources of revenue. Typically, states add their own taxes to the following:

- **Alcoholic beverage tax:** The range varies for various types of alcohol. This kind of tax is sometimes referred to as a "sin" tax.

- **Motor fuel tax:** All fuels used on public highways are subject to tax.

- **Motor vehicle registration tax:** A vehicle tax is imposed on automobiles, trucks, buses, tractors, motorcycles, semi trailers, and trailers for the privilege of using a motor vehicle in the state. These rates vary from state to state.

■ **Tobacco tax:** Both the federal and state governments impose a cigarette tax in an effort to reduce cigarette consumption. Taxes are also imposed on other tobacco products, such as cigars and chewing tobacco. The rates vary.

■ **Insurance tax:** Out-of-state companies and foreign companies doing insurance business within a state are subject to additional taxes for the privilege of doing business in that state. Basically, though, the taxes that any company — even in-state — pays for the privilege of doing business in a state are passed on to the consumer of its goods or services.

■ **Public utilities tax:** Suppliers of electricity, light, gas, and telecommunications within states are subject to various fees and taxes.

■ **Real estate transfer tax:** Many states charge a fee for buying and selling real estate, including your home. This tax is paid when the deed is recorded with the county.

Reducing How Much Tax You Pay

Although you can't spend all your time and energy looking for ways to avoid taxes, you can do some simple things to avoid paying more than you have to. Consider the following:

■ **Spend less.** You have to pay a sales tax on whatever you buy, but if you don't buy the most expensive items available, you don't pay the maximum taxes.

■ **Buy store brands.** Many items — whether premium or store brands — accomplish the same thing when used properly. Why pay a premium price for a disposable item and pay the additional tax that goes with it?

■ **Shop catalogs.** When you buy an item from a catalog, you often don't have to pay the state sales tax on that item. That's the good news; the bad news, however, is that you pay a shipping and handling charge that often exceeds what you would pay in state sales tax. You have to weigh one against the other.

■ **Barter.** As an individual, you may be able to trade one of your skills or services to another with a complementary skill or service. And if you can barter your plumbing skills for a friend's electrical skills, you can also avoid a cash transaction that requires a retail sales tax.

■ **Take advantage of coupons, discounts, and bargains.** If you have the time and inclination, you can buy just about everything you need to purchase at a cheaper price somewhere.

Avoiding Tax Trouble

No one wants to hassle with the IRS. Certain flags on a tax return increase your chances of being subject to an IRS examination, or *audit*. If you keep good records and file on time, you stand a good chance of steering clear of an IRS examination. But you do need to consider the clues that the IRS looks for.

Staying alert to audits

The IRS generally considers the following situations red flags:

■ Claiming more than 35 percent of adjusted gross income in itemized deductions

■ Claiming persons other than children, grandchildren, or parents as dependents and/or not providing dependents' social security numbers

■ Claiming large deductions for travel and entertainment not in proportion to income

■ Taking office-in-home deductions while employed elsewhere

■ Clues to unreported income, such as an unusually low income in the restaurant business

■ Underreporting tip income from businesses that receive gratuities

■ Claiming high interest deductions

■ Claiming bad debts

■ Taking large depreciation and maintenance deductions for rental property

■ Claiming high business use of a car in a business that traditionally doesn't have high car use

■ Claiming disproportionate charitable donations

You have no cause for panic when you're audited if you have calculated your taxes fairly and kept good records. And not all audits result in additional tax charges and penalties. If you are audited, you're responsible for substantiating your claims with sufficient records. In some cases, the IRS may simply request additional documentation or an explanation. In other cases, you may be called in for an audit, or the IRS may request a field audit at your place of business.

You have rights as a taxpayer, and the IRS is required to inform you of these rights before an audit. You can ask for more time to produce the required documentation and ask to stop the IRS interview so that you can consult with a tax adviser. You can bring an adviser or witness with you, and you can tape the interview. You also can appeal the audit findings.

The IRS must keep audit information confidential, but it may send your tax audit to your state tax authorities. If your audit results in changes to your federal tax report, you also have to make changes to your state tax report.

Doing the right thing

The complexities of tax law and tax reporting are daunting. Here are some tips for doing the right thing:

- **Be honest and fair.** Attempts to defraud the government by purposely giving false information about a significant tax issue are punishable.

- **Keep meticulous records.**

- **Order and use IRS documents and assistance.** Publication 17 (mentioned in Table 9-1) is especially important.

- **Pay for competence if you want someone to prepare your tax returns.** Tax preparers who are certified and sign your tax forms are generally more reliable than someone who has made a hobby of preparing tax forms. Go with the professionals; tax codes are complicated and you need the expertise of those who are informed with the current requirements. Ask your friends, family, or lawyer for tax preparer recommendations.

- **Use electronic filing for fast and accurate exchange of information with the IRS.** The benefits of electronic filing are many: The IRS confirms receipt of your return, so you don't have to wonder about mail delays. Electronic filing is more accurate because it eliminates data entry errors at the IRS. And if you're expecting a tax refund, you'll get it quicker.

CHAPTER 10

KEEPING IT ALL TOGETHER BY KEEPING RECORDS

IN THIS CHAPTER

- Saving time and frustration by getting organized
- Using files, folders, and forms for your financial records

Your role as a money manager will not seem so burdensome if you know that you have what you need to succeed. Why begin a money-management session with a sense of frustration because you can't find the information you want or need? Make it easy for yourself and use the information in this chapter to support your money-managing efforts.

Getting Organized

Getting organized is at least half the battle in developing money-management skills. If you just take the time, purchase a few supplies, and follow the simple steps identified in this section, you're on your way as a successful money manager. Make an appointment to meet with yourself every week — a short, half-hour meeting will do. Then every month, plan an extended appointment for which you allow an hour.

Getting started really doesn't take much. You need the following supplies to organize your financial records. If you don't have them, make a shopping list and go to the store:

- **Pens, pencils, paper, paper clips, and manila folders:** Tabbed folders let you see your records at a glance.

- **A file container:** You can use a cardboard box, a plastic crate, or a regular filing cabinet — whatever matches your budget.

- **Envelopes and postage stamps:** A box of business envelopes makes financial correspondence and payments easier. Have a supply of postage stamps on hand, too, so that you can be sure to make your payments on time.

- **An appointment book or notebook:** Record your business appointments and any expenditures that you can't track with receipts.

- **Software:** If you have a computer, programs such as Quicken and Microsoft Money can help you organize and track financial information.

Creating folders for keeping your financial records

Label a folder (include the year on the label) for each of the following items that applies to your financial situation. Put your folders in alphabetical order in your file container. Add additional folders as your situation calls for them.

- 401(k) or Keogh

- Automobile — Insurance and loan

- Automobile — Maintenance

- Bank accounts

- Charitable contributions

- Credit cards

- Educational records

- Health insurance

- Home — Improvements

- Home — Insurance

- Home — Mortgage

- Income tax — Federal

- Income tax — State

- Income tax — Local

- Insurance — Life and disability

- IRA

- Loan (specify type)

- Mutual funds

- Property tax bills

- Real estate (include your rental contract or mortgage information, tax information, and so on)

- Social security (include your number and any updates you receive regarding your projected retirement or disability income)

- Stocks

- Warranties

- Will and/or trust

Consolidate all the information you have and add it to each folder that pertains to that file. Record essential information on the cover of each folder. Identify the name, address, phone number, and policy number for each account, policy, or whatever. Collecting this information takes a little time but makes contacts and record keeping much easier over the course of the year.

Make copies of the forms in the following two worksheets. Fill in the information and staple them to the inside cover of the relevant folder. Some forms can do double duty.

Insurance (automobile, health, home, life, and disability):

Insurance company/ Financial institution _____

_____

Address _____

_____

Phone _____

Name of representative _____

Claim number _____

Policy number _____

Payments _____

Loan (car, mortgage, home equity):

Type of loan _____

Amount of loan _____

Interest rate on loan _____

Lending institution _____

Address _____

_____

Phone _____

Contact person _____

Date/Amount of payment _____

End of year balance _____

Tables 10-1 and 10-2 show other forms that you need to fill in. Staple the forms to the inside cover of the relevant folder.

Table 10-1: Banks and Credit Cards

Institution	Account Type	Account #	Interest Rate	Balance/Date	Contact Person	Address	Phone

Table 10-2: Stocks and Other Investments

Ticker Symbol	Date of Purchase	Number of Shares	Cost/ Share	Total Cost	Market Value/ Share	Total Market Value	Gain/Loss

These basic forms illustrate the kind of essential information for each of your folders. When you have information at your fingertips, you put it to better and more frequent use.

Keeping personal records

You'll also benefit from keeping personal information in one place. So while you're organizing, set up a personal file with the following information:

- **Social security number(s):** Include your social security number, as well as those of your spouse or partner, children, parents, and siblings.

- **Contact information:** List the names and addresses of each of your adult children and your parents. You may also want to include contact information for your siblings, spouse, trusted friends, and lawyer. Include work contact information when available.

- **Birth certificates:** Collect original birth certificates for each family member and keep them in this folder.

- **Marriage certificate/divorce decree:** Include your marriage certificate and/or divorce documents in your folder.

- **Personal will:** No matter what your age, make sure that you have an up-to-date will. If you already have a will, take another look at it see whether you need to make adjustments.

- **Living will:** You can ask your doctor to draw up a statement for a living will or pick up a form to fill out. Share this information with your family and keep a copy in your personal folder.

- **Passport or citizenship papers:** If you have a passport or citizenship papers, include these documents as well.

Because this information is so important and is difficult to replace, consider keeping your personal file in a safety deposit box at your bank or in a fireproof safe at home.

Staying Organized

Now that you've started the process of organizing your financial records, you want to stay on track. That means visiting your folders often and updating your financial information regularly. I recommend that you schedule a monthly appointment with yourself to help you stay organized and on track.

CLIFFSNOTES REVIEW

Use this CliffsNotes Review to practice what you've learned in this book and to build your confidence in doing the job right the first time. After you work through the review questions, the scenarios, and the fun and useful practice project, you're well on your way to achieving your goal of taking control of your money.

Q&A

1. Which of the following is *not* a money-management strategy?
   a. Achieving financial security
   b. Saving money
   c. Spending less than you earn

2. Your basic economic needs include
   a. Food, clothing, and vacations
   b. Housing, life insurance, and transportation
   c. Transportation, housing, and food

3. To save $1,000 a year, you can
   a. Postpone paying your bills
   b. Save $2.74 every day
   c. Ask your employer for a raise

4. Which of the following will *not* help you save money?
   a. Learning to live on less
   b. Subscribing to cable television
   c. Leaving your credit cards at home

5. When you have money to invest, which strategy works best?
   a. Buy undeveloped real estate far from where you live
   b. Diversify your investment portfolio
   b. Put it all in the bank

6. To maintain a good credit rating, you should

    a. Pay off the entire credit card balance when it is due

    b. Pay the minimum amount due each month

    c. Ignore the late charges if you think that they're not fair

7. Common sources of debt include

    a. Mortgages and home equity loans

    b. CDs and 401(k)s

    c. Cash and tips

8. The best advice about federal income taxes is

    a. File for an extension to delay payments

    b. Keep good records throughout the year

    c. Pay an expensive accountant to prepare your tax documents

Answers: 1. a. 2. c. 3. b. 4. b. 5. b. 6. a. 7. a. 8. b.

Scenarios

1. You're paying $800 a month for rent with a net income of $24,000 a year. You have the chance to move into a better apartment for $1,000 rent. You know that you'll need to replace your car within the year. Should you stay put or make the move?

_____

_____

2. You want to buy your first house and want to save $20,000 for your down payment. What three things can you do to make that a reality in three years?

_____

_____

Answers: 1. Apply the opportunity cost and benefit analysis to this situation. If you choose the more expensive apartment, you won't have as much money available for your car. 2. Set up a budget that enables you to save $7,000 a year by reducing your current spending on housing, transportation, and vacation costs. You can supplement your income with hobby income or a part-time job.

You can also allocate any bonus, tax refund, or gift money that you receive to a special house fund.

Consider This

- Did you know that by learning to live on less money, you can open the door to financial security through savings and investment? See Chapter 1 for tips.

- Did you know that managing your debt is as important as developing a savings plan? See Chapter 4 for practical suggestions for getting out of debt and Chapter 6 for money-saving tips.

Practice Project

1. Organize a storage box or file cabinet with labeled folders (such as those suggested in Chapter 10) to keep track of your financial records. Then go through your drawers and place the appropriate materials in the relevant folders. Customize forms for yourself that will help you keep track of the information you need to stay organized.

2. Take stock of the entire amount of debt you have. Add the total amounts for all student loans, cars, housing, installment payments, and credit cards. Develop a one-year, three-year, and five-year plan for reducing or eliminating your debts.

3. Practice investing an imaginary $10,000. First decide how you want to diversify your investment portfolio. Plan three investment strategies and plot the performance of all three over a period of six months to one year. Compare results at your monthly financial planning sessions.

CLIFFSNOTES RESOURCE CENTER

The learning doesn't stop here. CliffsNotes Resource Center shows you the very best of the best — links to the best information in print and online about taking control of your money. Look for these terrific resources at your favorite bookstore and on the Internet. When you're online, make your first stop www.cliffsnotes.com, because we've put together an even bigger CliffsNotes Resource Center there.

Books

This book is one of many great books on money management. If you want some great next-step books, check out some of these other publications:

- **Personal Finance For Dummies,** by Eric Tyson. Helps you with all the various aspects of money management: saving, investing, debt reduction, and so on. IDG Books Worldwide, Inc., $19.99.

- **CliffsNotes Investing for the First Time,** by Tracey Longo. Helps you figure out how to break into the world of investing after you take control of your financial affairs. IDG Books Worldwide, Inc., $8.99.

- **Investing Online For Dummies,** by Kathleen Sindell, Ph.D. Shows you how to take advantage of all the investing opportunities that the Internet has to offer. IDG Books Worldwide, Inc., $24.99.

- **Home Buying For Dummies**, by Eric Tyson and Ray Brown. Introduces you to the world of real estate agents, mortgages, escrow, and more and helps you get the best deal on your dream home. IDG Books Worldwide, Inc., $16.99.

- **Taxes For Dummies,** by Eric Tyson. Helps you reduce your tax burden and makes preparing tax returns a snap. IDG Books Worldwide, Inc., $16.99.

It's easy to find books published by IDG Books Worldwide, Inc. You'll find them in your favorite bookstores (on the Internet and at stores near you). We also have three Web sites that you can use to read about all the books we publish:

- `www.cliffsnotes.com`
- `www.dummies.com`
- `www.idgbooks.com`

Internet

Check out these Web sites for more information about taking control of your money — and what to do with it once you gain that control:

- **Rate.net, www.rate.net** — This site is the largest index of rates, tracking 11,000 financial institutions and updating 100,000 rates weekly.

- **Financenter, www.financenter.com/budget.htm** — This site includes calculators to help you determine rates for auto loans, home mortgages, and credit cards. It also provides information about credit lines, insurance, budgeting, and retirement.

- **Bankrate.com, www.bankrate.com** — This site includes average rates for credit cards as well as checking and ATM fees. It also offers assistance for small businesses and online finances and will give the information in Spanish if you prefer.

- **Cheapskate Monthly, www.cheapskatemonthly.com** — A folksy and informative collection of tips for living frugally.

- **Quicken, www.quicken.com** — This site provides stock quotes in addition to informative features and departments.

- **New York Stock Exchange www.nyse.com** — This is the place to go for stock information. The site includes a glossary for those who want to get to the meaning of it all.

- **Money Rates, www.money-rates.com** — This site provides information about the national averages for CDs, Treasury bonds, money market accounts, and mortgage rates. A good general reference for consumer rates and bank rates.

- **Armchair Millionaire, www.armchairmillionaire. com** — This site offers attractive features, including Five Steps to Financial Freedom. It has partnered with Quicken and provides an Investor Center in collaboration with Charles Schwab.

Next time you're on the Internet, don't forget to drop by www.cliffsnotes.com. We created an online Resource Center that you can use today, tomorrow, and beyond.

Send Us Your Favorite Tips

In your quest for learning, have you ever experienced that sublime moment when you figure out a trick that saves time or trouble? Perhaps you realized you were taking ten steps to accomplish something that could have taken two. Or you found a little-known workaround that gets great results. If you've discovered a useful tip that helped you budget more effectively and you'd like to share it, the CliffsNotes staff would love to hear from you. Go to our Web site at www.cliffsnotes.com and click the Talk to Us button. If we select your tip, we may publish it as part of CliffsNotes Daily, our exciting, free e-mail newsletter. To find out more or to subscribe to a newsletter, go to www.cliffs-notes.com on the Web.

INDEX

NUMBERS

COMING SOON FROM CLIFFSNOTES

COMING SOON FROM CLIFFSNOTES
Buying and Selling on eBay

Have you ever experienced the thrill of finding an incredible bargain at a specialty store or been amazed at what people are willing to pay for things that you might toss in the garbage? If so, then you'll want to learn about eBay — the hottest auction site on the Internet. And CliffsNotes *Buying and Selling on eBay* is the shortest distance to eBay proficiency. You'll learn how to:

- Find what you're looking for, from antique toys to classic cars
- Watch the auctions strategically and place bids at the right time
- Sell items online at the eBay site
- Make the items you sell attractive to prospective bidders
- Protect yourself from fraud

Here's an example of how the step-by-step CliffsNotes learning process simplifies placing a bid at eBay:

1. Scroll to the Web page form that is located at the bottom of the page on which the auction item itself is presented.

2. Enter your registered eBay username and password and enter the amount you want to bid. A Web page appears that lets you review your bid before you actually submit it to eBay. After you're satisfied with your bid, click the Place Bid button.

3. Click the Back button on your browser until you return to the auction listing page. Then choose View⇨Reload (Netscape Navigator) or View⇨Refresh (Microsoft Internet Explorer) to reload the Web page information. Your new high bid appears on the Web page, and your name appears as the high bidder.